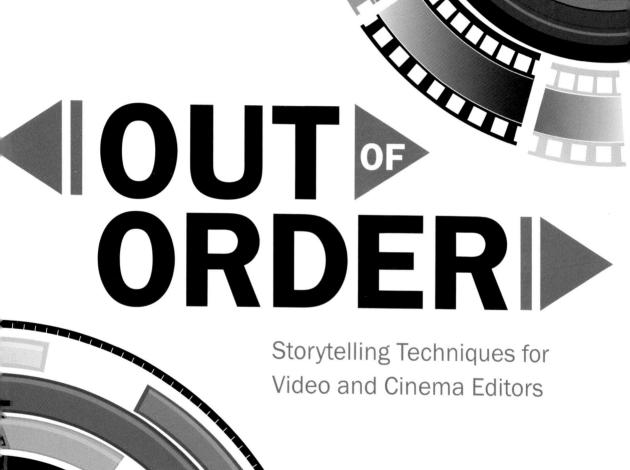

◀| OUT ▶|OF▶ ORDER|▶

Storytelling Techniques for
Video and Cinema Editors

▶ **Ross Hockrow**

◎ PEACHPIT PRESS

Out of Order: Storytelling Techniques for Video and Cinema Editors
Ross Hockrow

Peachpit Press
Find us on the Web at www.peachpit.com

To report errors, please send a note to errata@peachpit.com
Peachpit Press is a division of Pearson Education

Senior Editor: Karyn Johnson
Development Editor: Corbin Collins
Production Editor: Danielle Foster
Technical Editor: Justin Edelman
Copyeditor: Kelly Kordes Anton
Compositor: David Van Ness
Proofreader: Liz Welch
Indexer: Valerie Haynes Perry
Interior Design: Danielle Foster
Cover Design: Aren Howell Straiger

Notice of Rights

Notice of Liability

Trademarks

ISBN-13: 978-0-321-95160-1
ISBN-10: 0-321-95160-3

9 8 7 6 5 4 3 2 1

Printed and bound in the United States of America

About the Author

Ross Hockrow is an acclaimed filmmaker, innovative educator, and published author. He has directed six feature-length films and several award-winning short films, the latest of which won the Audience Choice Award for the 2013 48-Hour Film Festival in Providence, Rhode Island, and Philadelphia, Pennsylvania.

Hockrow's filmmaking abilities stretch beyond narratives and into commercial work for the Fortune 500 companies Skype and Expedia. He also directed a promotional piece featuring Bill Gates. An Adobe-sponsored speaker and editor, he pioneered live filmmaking education with his Get In Motion tour in 2011—the industry's first-ever educational workshop tour created exclusively for filmmakers.

Hockrow has lectured in more than 100 cities during three international tours, and he has taught platform classes at several major industry tradeshows, including NAB, CES, and WPPI. In 2014, he was selected to teach the first-ever filmmaking course on the CreativeLIVE online learning platform; the course attracted over 40,000 viewers. Hockrow's well-received first book, *Storytelling Techniques for Digital Filmmakers* (Amherst Media, 2013), led to a follow-up book on editing theory, which you now hold in your hands. He recently completed the Out of Order tour, dedicated to the Out of Order brand, which involves a feature film, this book, and continuing education.

Acknowledgments

A great deal of time, effort, and brain power went into writing this book. First, I want to say that five years ago I started a mission. I was a young, self-taught filmmaker who relied solely on my editing skills to be a good filmmaker. When I started out, editing was really the only thing I could control from a budgetary standpoint because it was just my brain and the computer. Camera and lenses didn't matter once the footage was shot. Needless to say, I was a terrible director when I first started out, but I saved many projects with editing. As I improved as a director, I realized how much editing really shaped who I was as a filmmaker. I worked backwards. I became a great editor first, and then slowly worked my way backwards to an understanding of filmmaking after seeing the elements I needed on the editing board. Eventually, it all clicked.

Clay Blackmore and Jeff Medford offered my first opportunity to teach editing. In my first tour of teaching photographers this new DSLR technology, I realized everyone was very scared of editing. I didn't understand why at first, and then I perceived a massive misunderstanding of editing. Because I was teaching photographers to be filmmakers, their natural assumption was that editing film was equivalent to using Photoshop to fine-tune images. But those two things couldn't be more different. I made it my mission to make people see what editing really is and understand that it is controlled by the brain via the choices you make while editing.

I can honestly say that I have accomplished that mission after three nationwide tours, a CreativeLive appearance, and many conventions and master classes. None of that really compares to this book, however. This book is part of a brand dubbed Out of Order, which includes the movie that comes with the book and a tour (which, sorry, already happened). This book is everything I believe editors need to focus on. For some, it represents an adjustment to the way they think. It's a little bit like finding out the world is round when for so long you *knew* it was flat. Don't worry, you'll get used to it.

This book would not have been possible without the people around me helping me do this. The first person I want to thank is Corbin Collins. It's funny because we've never met in person, but he was assigned to be the editor for this book. When I submitted the first chapter to him and he told me to rewrite it, I felt like a 22-year-old punk all over again (although it wasn't that long ago—I'm now 28). I said to myself, "What does this guy know?" Then I reread his notes and realized, "This is the guy who is going to make this a book." Not me. I just know things. Articulating those things into coherent sentences so that people can actually understand what I'm saying is a skill, and I didn't realize how hard it is. I started out in this business as a scriptwriter, but writing a book is a totally different animal. Corbin pushed me to the limit with every word, sentence, and description, and this book is just as much his as it is mine. Without him, no one would understand what I'm actually saying.

Secondly, I want to thank Karyn Johnson for giving me the opportunity to write this book. As hard as it was, it was a pleasure, and without Karyn none of this would have ever happened. Karyn could have selected any one of several filmmakers, and even more teachers, out there. But she chose me. I hope this book reassures that choice. And thanks to Kelly Kordes Anton, our copyeditor, who fixed and polished the final product.

Next, I want to thank Jeff Medford and Clay Blackmore for finding me in in the University of Delaware library (illegally). I was editing low-budget rap videos, and they gave me the opportunity to actually make a living being a filmmaker. As I sit in my new house, only two days old, I can't help but think that without those guys I'd still be sneaking into the U of D library and editing videos for $100. I will forever be in their debt.

I want to dedicate this book to my dog Cleveland. Really? Am I going there? Yes, but hear me out. Nine years ago, after playing high-stakes professional poker for three years, I decided to take all of my money and start my film career. I thought, "Why not? I have so much of it, what could go wrong?" Well, movies cost a lot to make, and I didn't know how much until I burned through all of it.

When I met Cleveland, he was suffering from an undiagnosed sickness that no vet could seem to figure out. Before I made any films, I spent countless dollars trying to figure out what was wrong with this pup. Finally, we found someone who knew. From that point on, Cleveland and I were inseparable. He sat at my feet for every mouse click as I edited seven feature films; dozens of short, feature documentaries; music videos; commercials; and everything under the sun. I brought him to shoots, meetings, and even coffee shops to write.

Sadly, on January 10, 2014, he was diagnosed with Stage 4 lung cancer. The vets said he would be dead within two weeks. I thought to myself, "Cleveland is a badass 100 pound pitbull, and nothing on the planet can kill him in 14 days." Sure, I've saved his life, but he's saved mine twice as well. Once we were hiking in a swampy park when a snake popped out of nowhere, hissing; within seconds, the snake was dismantled and we were on our way. The second time, we were attacked by a wild dog during a walk, and I almost lost my right hand. Cleveland fought off the dog and stayed with me until help came. After 22 stitches, I was back to editing that night.

But all good things must come to an end, and 48 hours from now my best friend will be put to sleep. The date is May 23, 2014, and he long exceeded his 14-day death sentence. I'm dedicating this book to him because it's the last project for which he sat at my feet while I wrote, edited, or just thought. I haven't made a film without him being there for some part of the process, and this project is our final one together.

Contents

Prologue

You might be asking yourself, "Prologue? Why is there a prologue in a book about editing video?" This isn't exactly *Game of Thrones* here. It's a fair question. Or maybe you're asking the question I always ask myself when I open a book with a prologue: "Do I have to read this?" In this case, the answer is yes. This might be the single most important text you'll read in this entire book. Before we even begin to examine the psychological filmmaking enigma that goes by the misleading name of *editing*, we must first explore exactly what the goal of editing really is. I understand that I'm going a bit out of order here...pun intended...but this is the way it needs to be.

ABOUT THIS BOOK

As you can see from the first several sentences, this isn't your traditional, click-here, drag-here, move-this-there type of book. The purpose of this book, and the "out of order" concept in general, is to teach you how to approach editing primarily through storytelling. You'll find this book is written as if the information, in and of itself, is a story. It builds upon past knowledge as it lays the foundation of central concepts. Before we can lay down that foundation, though, we need to get a few things straight.

There is a huge misconception that editing is primarily a technical skill. It's viewed as a sort of trade that requires the same commitment to training as, say, a massage therapist or nurse. I strongly disagree. While much of the editing training available does rely heavily on a how-to approach, these tangible skills don't make you a good editor. You learn a little editing theory, but a lot about technical issues such as the editing process, types of cuts, how to make cuts, file compression, color correction, and basic navigation of an editing program. The best thing you can do to be a great editor, however, is learn how to *think*. The smartest scientist in the world is much more useful if he or she knows how to conduct an experiment. Knowing the ins and outs of an editing program makes you no more than a technical advisor. Although it's a respectable calling card, and there are many jobs in the industry for what we call postproduction supervisors, it's not the reason you picked up this book. The difference between an editor and a postproduction supervisor is that the postproduction supervisor sees things in a technical language—a very black-and-white approach to editing—whereas the editor sees many shades of gray. A good editor sees things that are open to interpretation and change.

Now, of course, technical-minded editors have overseen amazing works of art, but without using methods of storytelling in the edit room, they are merely messengers. They follow a script. If a script is good, the pieces are well shot, and the director has vision...well, two plus two usually equals four. However, an editor who approaches the process correctly, with the mind of storyteller, can always add something to a film, and any good director would welcome such an upgrade. And if you're usually the one doing it all—directing, conceptualizing, editing—then being able to think like an editor is all the more important. I hope reading this book forever changes your entire approach to editing.

EDITING, OLD AND NEW

Before digital filmmaking became popular, or even possible, things were done on film. The process of putting together a film is now much, much easier. Today, anyone can use Adobe Premiere Pro or Final Cut Pro. But before that, filmmaking was much more difficult. There was an actual craft in cutting film. Sometimes, the best editor was a combination of the mind and the craft. Now, it's just the mind.

Many more editors are working now than back in 1970. It's evolution. The more people *can* do it, the more people *will* do it, and the better the competition. This competition breeds better editors, leading to better final results. I could teach my dog to push buttons on a keyboard. What I can't teach my dog is to see a film in thousands of pieces, and within those pieces, look at the chaos and the infinite combinations for arranging those pieces to tell hundreds of versions of the same story. And I certainly can't teach my dog to spot that one perfect final result. That is one of the secrets of editing. Always know the direction you're traveling. You rarely want to begin editing and not be sure of the final result you're trying to achieve.

It's very much like driving. Whether you're going to the store, the beach, or on a long trip, what matters is how you get there. There are a few ways to get to the store, more ways to reach the beach, and going on a road trip brings in new variables such as traffic and weather. Do you see where I'm going with this analogy? Once you decide on a destination, there are many ways to get there. So how do driving and filmmaking in 1970 tie in with the editing approach? Keep reading.

Somewhere between 1990 and 2000, editing became a digital process. Even when shooting on film, editors would convert it to digital, edit it, and then convert it back to film for print. My big problem with this era is that no one bothered to step back and look at what happened. We changed the process of editing. We digitized it and made it faster, easier, and more accessible—yet we still think about it in the same way.

Does that seem wrong to anyone else? Back to the driving analogy: In that same time span, we went from paper maps and asking for directions at gas stations to MapQuest and eventually GPS. Makes traveling more efficient, doesn't it?

Now that editing is more efficient, you can keep your eye on the prize, which is getting the most out of your footage. The first step to getting the most out of your footage is getting the most of out of *you*. Crafting a story is not something you should be doing while tired, angry, frustrated, or in the thrall of any other negative emotion. You need to take a Zen-like approach. Your energy, whatever energy you're feeling at the time, will translate into your film. If you don't believe that statement, please take my word for it.

GROOVE AND FLOW

You need to find what I call the *editing groove*. Once you find that groove, you should not get up from your computer for any reason unless absolutely necessary. What is the groove? It sounds like some made-up BS concept designed to be motivational. Maybe. But I believe it's real, and it's possible today because the computer puts your clips and everything else you need right at your fingertips. If you were cutting film, that wouldn't be possible. This single fact, to me, changes the results you can get from footage and makes editing *better*. The groove happens when you're consistently thinking creatively instead of constantly worrying about technical skills such as cutting film.

Once you've decided on a direction for your story, or an editing style for something involving a script, you'll begin editing. Where to physically start is something I discuss in the book, but once you begin editing, you'll start to gain a *flow*. That is, as you craft your film, scene, short story, documentary, whatever it is, it will start to take shape. One of three things will happen:

1. That film will take shape and be exactly what you envisioned it to be.

2. The film will take shape, and you'll see that the direction or style needs to be altered in order to achieve that quality you were originally hoping for.

3. The film will start to take shape, but you can see it's not working, forcing you to start over and go in a new direction. Editing is a lot of trial and error as far as assembling pieces in the proper order.

None of the three options is better than the others, nor does one have a higher success rate, but each offers a clear visual of what your film is going to be. Once you've seen that visual, you'll finally be creating based on something real rather than hypothetical.

TIP *It's easier to modify something that exists than to create something from nothing.*

You'll find the philosophy behind that tip laced throughout this book because it applies to several aspects of the editing process. The point is that once you're in the *modifying* stage, that's when the groove begins. And when the groove begins, you want to extend moments of enlightenment as long as you possibly can because those are, by far, the most valuable editing hours. When I hit my groove, I do not get up until a rough cut of a short film or scene is completed.

I used to say that editing is like a puzzle, and no one in his or her right mind would try to solve a puzzle without the picture on the box for reference. As I developed my own editing skills and style, I realized that statement was misleading. Sure, editing is like a puzzle in the sense that you're combining pieces into a final masterpiece, but editing has a few major differences. One of those differences is that you'll only use 10–20 percent of the pieces you have. Puzzles would be a lot more challenging if they included a bunch of pieces you don't need! Another difference is that the image on the outside of the puzzle box is set in stone while an image of a film in your head can change like the wind. And lastly, just because a piece fits perfectly in a spot doesn't mean it won't fit perfectly elsewhere. That's something most puzzles cannot boast.

There is a psychological variable to every edit, and a lot of that comes down to pace and rhythm (which are also discussed in this book). The key is to open your mind to what editing truly is and understand that the variables involved will make or break your entire film. Think about it this way. I could give the same footage to four different editors and get four different products. But let's go further. It doesn't have to be an event film, a wedding video, or a documentary for which the editor crafts the story on the editing board with someone else's captured footage. I could give a scripted conversation between two characters in a film to those same four editors and still get four different scenes. How? Emotion and pace. In editing, it's the little things that make the world of difference. These include knowing when to cut to a facial expression, leave a breath of air between words, close the gap and speed up the dialogue, and cut a meaningless line. Little things also include knowing when and where to use close-ups and how long to hold a shot. Sure, the words spoken will be the same, but the feeling each editor gives the viewers, and the entertainment value and interest they command, will be drastically different.

CONVERSATION IS THE FOUNDATION OF EDITING

When I started as a filmmaker, I dove right into feature filmmaking by writing and directing my first film. I was 20 years old and knew nothing about being a filmmaker. I only knew I had *ideas* (who doesn't?). Ideas are one thing, but execution is something else entirely. Because of the low-budget nature of this film, it was a dialogue-heavy narrative. One scene from the climax, a conversation between two people, was nine pages long. The general rule is that a page of dialogue in a script translates to about a minute on film. We were looking at a nine-minute conversation! Much too long. While editing this scene, my co-editor and I sat in the University of Delaware library for weeks (we weren't students, we just snuck in with fake IDs to use their state-of-the-art editing suite). We tried different ways to cut the scene and nothing worked. My co-editor suggested cutting the scene from the film completely. I'll never forget what he said: "If the beginning of the movie is good, and the end of the movie is good, but you hate the middle, then start cutting things from the middle." Interesting—and correct—concept, but it was the wrong time to apply it. I suggested a compromise. We reduced that nine-minute scene to six minutes. To this day, it's one of the best conversations I've edited in my career. Guess what we cut out by getting rid of three minutes?

Nothing.

Not one line was sacrificed. Not one facial expression was sacrificed. In that session, we learned that a conversation in the real world, a conversation on paper, and a conversation on film are three totally different animals. It was then that I realized that the *conversation* is the foundation for all of editing. Once you understand how to cut a conversation, you'll be able to edit anything. You'll be able to see the final structure of a film even before it's shot. These are the phenomena we will explore in this book.

Now, everything you think you know about editing—how to edit, the way you personally edit, or whatever you've heard—forget it. I want you to learn the information in the exact order in which it appears in this book. Chapter 1 is about the story arc, and it's your foundation. In every chapter after that, you'll be adding information to your current knowledge. Treat it as if it's a puzzle. The more pieces you place, the clearer the picture gets. If you can do that and add pieces to the puzzle as they are explained in this book, in a designed order, you'll be an editor by the time you get to the back cover. Not only will you be an editor, but you'll improve every time you edit, because you'll take each experience and add it as a lesson.

So, in the true nature of *Out of Order...* in Chapter 1, let's go all the way back to the beginning and answer the single most important question: "What is a story?"

ACCESSING THE DOWNLOADS FOR THIS BOOK

Out of Order isn't just a book—it's also a movie! The film is a character study drama about the invention of digitized editing. It was created for two purposes: for entertainment and to create scenes that can be used as examples to teach the theories discussed in this book.

Buying this book gives you access to two films of mine, a short film called *The Pre-Nup* and the full-length feature film *Out of Order*. The audio narration version of *Out of Order* is referred to throughout this book, with timecodes included so you can fast-forward or rewind directly to the relevant section.

To access the downloads to this book, please follow these steps:

1. On a Mac or PC, go to www.peachpit.com/redeem.

2. Enter this code: 8C3E33623F09.

3. If you do not have a Peachpit.com account, you will be prompted to create one.

4. The downloadable files will be listed under the Lesson & Update Files tab on your Account page.

5. Click the file links to download them to your computer.

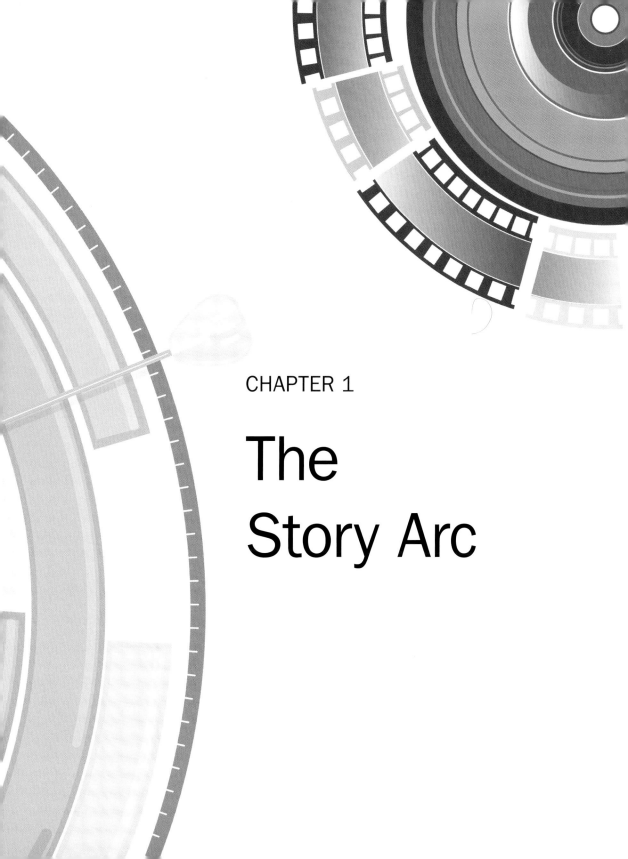

CHAPTER 1

The
Story Arc

You might be asking yourself, why are we starting with a film's story arc? Isn't this the writer's job? Yes, it's certainly a concern for the writer or the person conceptualizing the story for your film. However, if you're reading this book, nowadays chances are you have your hand in all aspects of filmmaking. You come up with the ideas. You shoot the footage needed to assemble the film. You know a little bit about lighting. You're editing, color correcting, and mixing audio. You might even be visiting third-party websites to find music to score your film.

Chances are you have your hand in all aspects of filmmaking.

If this is you, you're certainly not alone. This scenario is a sign of the times—and of technology. In the past 5 to 10 years, high-quality filmmaking has gone from being accessible only with a Hollywood budget to being available to anyone with HD video on a smartphone. It's a new world in filmmaking.

This may be good news for anyone trying to produce high-quality films that were previously only possible with millions of dollars, but there's also a catch: You should know how to complete every part of the filmmaking process.

Look at postproduction. In the past, there was an editor, a few assistant editors, a colorist, a sound engineer, a postproduction supervisor, a music supervisor, a Foley artist, a dailies editor, and the list goes on. That's a lot of jobs, a lot of people, and a lot of very expensive computer systems.

> **NOTE** *Nowadays, in most cases, a filmmaking operation is one person, doing many jobs, on a very powerful laptop. This is just the way things are in the state of filmmaking today.*

Today, you'll likely be wearing a lot of hats. That's why I'm starting you off on your journey to learn editing theory with a foundation in storytelling: the story arc. You may be coming up with your own stories, or maybe you truly are only the editor on a project.

Why the Story Arc Is So Important

Regardless of how many hats you wear as a filmmaker, the story should constantly be on your mind. Consideration of the story arc should be present in every decision you'll ever make. As an editor, you're always feeding the story arc.

That means this is, in many ways, the most important chapter of this book. I say this for three reasons:

1. The plot structure of the story will influence your editing decision making.

2. Knowing where you are in the story arc is very important while editing.

3. The story arc is everywhere. It's in the large scale of the overall story and it goes all the way down to the smallest scale when it's used in the context of assembling two shots.

A story arc is similar to a roller coaster. It starts stationary and flat. It rises to a climax, and then it falls to an inevitable resolution. Like a story, the roller coaster can begin a few ways. Here are just a couple:

- The arc can rise slowly, beginning and developing at a modest pace. It relies on the facts you chose to be a part of the story and doesn't need to come out of the gates intense. It develops methodically. This refers to the overall story, which the writer is responsible for in a scripted story, and is mirrored in the editing process with cutting speed, known as *pacing*. (Pacing is the timing of the cuts when changing from one clip to the other. See Chapter 4 for more on pacing.)

- The arc can rise quickly, launching out of the gates with a bang. Maybe the roller coaster takes off and relies on the element of surprise or disorientation to draw you into the story, which means speeding up the pace.

In any event, the story arc influences decisions from top to bottom when it comes to editing.

Ignoring the story arc can put you in guessing mode when it comes time to edit. If you guess wrong about where you are in the story, you can end up giving out incorrect information to your viewers. Providing inaccurate information or delivering information in the wrong order can result in the viewers "checking out" and ignoring the story altogether. Ignoring the story arc also puts you in a guessing mode when it comes to things such as pacing and shot selection.

NOTE Understanding the story arc offers a clear-cut way to take your editing to another level. It allows you to incorporate how the viewer's mind works into every choice you make while editing.

Nothing you do in editing is random. Everything you do is for a purpose. **FIGURE 1.1** shows what a story arc, also sometimes called a plot structure, looks like. You should try to implant it in your mind. (Bear in mind that it seems like a film's climax occurs more toward the end, and that is sometimes the case. However, the climax usually occurs around the two-thirds mark of a film. Figure 1.1 shows the up and down shape of the story arc.)

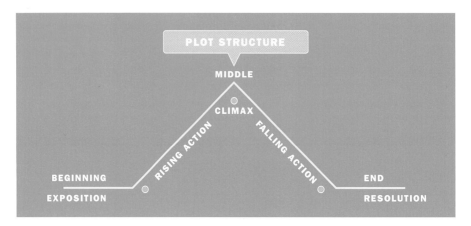

FIGURE 1.1 A modern-day story arc is broken into five parts. This represents the overall story, but inside each scene you'll find story arcs as well. The arc is also known as a *flip*.

Every story is loosely divided into three acts:

- Act 1 is the exposition.
- Act 2 is the rising action, the climax, and the falling action.
- Act 3 is the resolution.

The story arc itself, sometimes known as the plot arc, consists of five parts:

- The exposition (beginning) is one of the two flat points of the plot arc.
- The rising action is where the anticipation builds.
- The climax (middle) is where the film turns the corner—not necessarily in terms of the running time of your story, but in terms of the middle portion of the arc. The "middle" or climax of a story can come 30 minutes into a

60-minute film, or 45 minutes into a 60-minute film. It's not about time, but the arrangement of the events in the story. In that sense, the climax is the middle of the story.

- The falling action, represented by the down slope, mirrors the rising action.

- The resolution (ending) is where you wrap up your story, usually in a clean and concise way.

Breaking Down Story Arcs

Even novice filmmakers are likely to know that every story has an arc, but it doesn't stop there. Yes, every complete story has an arc—but so does every *scene* in every story. Think about each scene, or "moment," in your film as its own mini film, with its own plot arc. The difference between the overall story arc and the individual scene arc is that the scene arc feeds into the next scene in a seamless fashion, all while feeding the main story.

Video Example: *The Pre-Nup*

While I'd love to make an analogy to a famous feature film here (and in the book many times that will be the case), the big arc/little arc reference can be explored by reviewing a short film. To better understand it, please take seven minutes to watch a film I created called *The Pre-Nup*. You can download it (and other materials for this book) from the publisher's site. See the sidebar, "Accessing the Downloads for This Book," for details. If you currently don't have access to the film, you can still follow along.

▶ **ACCESSING THE DOWNLOADS FOR THIS BOOK**

Purchasing this book gives you access to two films I created, a short film called *The Pre-Nup* and a full-length feature film called *Out of Order*, a story of the man who invented the first digitized nonlinear editing system. The audio narration version of *Out of Order* is referred to throughout this book, with relevant timecodes included. Please see this book's Introduction for instructions on downloading the files.

First let's identify the major plot arc of *The Pre-Nup*. It's broken into five parts, known as *plot points*. I explore those five parts and their purposes in detail later in this chapter. For now, talking about *The Pre-Nup*, it's only the events that matter:

1. **Exposition:** A man breaks into a house and steals a bunch of jewelry. An unrelated couple is shown fighting before getting into a car. Those are two separate actions, two separate scenes. They are both part of the exposition plot point of the story. The *exposition* is another word for the beginning. You'll see why all this makes up the exposition when I dissect the exposition later in this chapter.

2. **Rising action:** The man attempts to steal a television, but he is interrupted by a knock at the door. The Publishers Clearing House shows up to give the owner of the house 10 million dollars. Again, two different actions that make up the rising action's plot point of the arc.

3. **Climax:** We find out the couple who was fighting in the beginning are the occupants of the house. The couple shows up while the burglar pretends to be Philip Reed, who is the real owner of the house.

4. **Falling action:** After an awkward encounter, the real Philip Reed gets rid of the burglar, dumps his girlfriend, and keeps the money for himself.

5. **Resolution:** The girlfriend and the burglar end up dating while Philip Reed thrives as a rich man.

That's an example of the plot arc. It requires a storytelling and writing skill set. When a writer creates a story, the writer follows the arc as a method to organize the story and keep it moving in the right direction. The first thing I do when I write a script is draw a picture of the arc, as shown in Figure 1.1, and notate the plot points that go in each part. In fact, this breakdown of *The Pre-Nup* is exactly how I mapped out the film before I wrote the script.

Now, this is not a book on writing; this is a book on editing. But editing involves a lot of storytelling—and storytelling is directly linked to script writing. In filmmaking, especially nowadays, everything connects. No part of the process is separate. In the modern world, as I said earlier, most filmmakers do all the jobs. If you're an event filmmaker, say, or you have a company that does commercials, chances are you write, direct, shoot, and edit. This makes the plot arc even more important. If you understand the plot arc concept and the other editing theories covered in this book, that knowledge will start to influence the shots you choose to get while filming. In addition, it will influence the ideas you come up with on your own. When you understand how the puzzle is put together—which is what editing is—you get a better sense of what puzzle pieces you need. Creating all the other puzzles pieces you need makes up every other part of filmmaking. As an editor, it's your job to weave the plot points together in a way that keeps the viewers on the roller coaster.

Drilling Down to Smaller Arcs

The five points discussed previously are the primary story arc, but now let's focus on one plot point. How about number one, the exposition. That plot point has its *own* five-point plot arc in *The Pre-Nup*:

1. A man attempts to break into a house.
2. After several failed attempts, he breaks into the back door and enters the house.
3. He finds jewelry, and then sees a television he really wants.
4. We see an unrelated couple fighting before getting into a car.
5. The first man is stealing the television, and is then interrupted by someone knocking at the door.

That arc is only the arc of the very first plot point in the bigger arc. It doesn't stop there. Take plot point three of the smaller arc. He sees a television he wants very badly. This can be broken down further into *another* arc:

1. The man sees something that catches his eye. He's mesmerized by what he sees.
2. We see it's a television.
3. He grabs the television.

That is a three-point plot arc. The five-point arc has more buildup and wind-down, but they are both arcs.

Connecting Arcs to Take the Viewers on a Ride

How does all this affect editing? If you switch plot point one with plot point two in the smallest arc (the third one), your arc is broken. There's no longer a need for you, the editor, to ever show the man's expression when he sees the television in the first place. The whole idea of the character seeing the television, without our knowing what he's looking at, is to draw us in. Making that happen is as simple as the ordering of two shots on the editing board. (The editing board is also known as a *timeline*. This is where you arrange the clips for your film.) This may seem like a small choice in the grand scheme of editing a film, but these choices add up to be the difference between a well-told story and one that doesn't translate well or benefit from the editing process.

Let's go back to plot point five in the second arc. The burglar has the television in hand and then there is a knock on the door. We as the audience are already transitioning ourselves into the next plot arc: Who is at the door? Editing each moment or scene must be thought about and done in a way that leads the viewers from one arc into the next. If you lay out a few story arcs from a film one after the other, you'll notice they make what looks like a very exciting roller coaster or the blips on a heart rate monitor.

This captures the entire idea of stories in general. You're trying to take the viewers on a ride, and the plot arc is the emotional shape of that ride. When you hear *emotional shape*, think of several plot arcs next to each other. Try imagining that as a heart rate monitor. The only consistency of the heart rate monitor is that the lines go up and down. How high and how low depend to some extent on emotion—how fast your heart is beating. Try thinking of a story as a constant heart rate monitor with the goal of changing the viewer's heart rate at will. This will be important when we get to pacing in Chapter 4. For now, think of things like the heart rate monitor and the roller coaster as metaphors for all the arcs present in the story.

Keep in mind: There is nothing exciting about a roller coaster that only goes up, or one that only drops. It's the slow rise that makes the drop fun. In film theory, we call this the *buildup*.

Reveals

The buildup can involve what's known as a *reveal*. Most stories have a major reveal in the big story arc, but your goal is to litter the smaller arcs with reveals as well. Again, you are at the whim of the script, but as the editor it's your job to get these reveals across the way they are intended. For example, in Video 1.1 (*The Pre-Nup*), when there is a knock at the door, the burglar looks out the window and you can kind of see who is outside. Wouldn't it have been more effective to never show who is outside? Then, when the door opens, it would be a bigger surprise. You're right. I put that in the film to illustrate how one simple insertion of a shot can damage the reveal.

Of course, other factors come into play here, such as narrative perspective. The *narrative perspective* refers to what perspective the story is told from (that's explored in Chapter 3). Speaking strictly from the standpoint of a reveal, that shot is a mistake. Delete that shot from the film, and the moment feels more like a reveal.

Anticipation

The conditions the filmmaker sets for the story creates anticipation in the viewer's mind. These conditions may include the setting, mood, character, or any element that you establish in the beginning. In terms of this example, what if I showed a shot of New York City to establish the setting? Your mind will connect your own personal experiences with New York City, or lack thereof, and you will now be participating in telling the story. That participation adds to the anticipation.

Something happens in the viewer's brain while observing these conditions. The viewers start to process and anticipate. Once viewers start to process, they lead themselves into the next part of the story. In *The Pre-Nup*, the moment you hear a knock at the door, you immediately start to speculate about who might be knocking. Your first instinct is that it's the couple you saw earlier in the film. Or maybe it's the police. It doesn't matter—once the knock happens, the viewers shift to thinking about the next part of the arc.

As an editor, always keep in mind that storytelling is a collaboration between the filmmaker and the viewer. It's the filmmaker's job to come up with the story. The viewer's job is to hit play and follow the story. The editor's job is to present the pieces in the proper order that makes the film feel like an experience, not just a movie.

This chapter explores the story arc in detail so you can begin to incorporate the benefits of story anticipation into your film editing. In later chapters, you'll put this to work, creating anticipation by putting shots back to back.

It's all about the viewer's mind. Let's explore what happens to viewers when they follow a story onscreen.

Story Arc and the Viewer

We as humans are wired to expect stories. We need them. We are born wanting stories. Every child loves a good bedtime story. Likewise, when the viewers press play, they want to love your film. They want to be influenced or touched by your story. A huge factor in whether your story works on that level is *how* you give the information to the viewer.

The Ancient Roots of Story

The story arc is not something Hollywood created, nor is it new. Aristotle first conceptualized it as a three-point plot structure around 335 B.C. (**FIGURE 1.2**). It looks like a triangle, with the triangle's points representing the beginning, middle, and end.

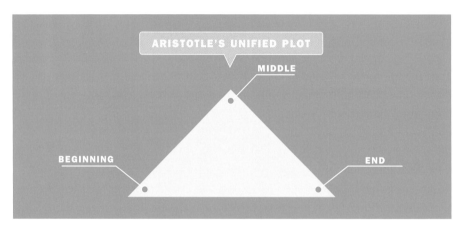

FIGURE 1.2 The plot arc as Aristotle conceptualized it. It's not far off from what it looks like today. Some smaller arcs buried deep inside scenes use a plot arc that looks like this, too.

More than 2,000 years later, in the 1860s, novelist and playwright Gustav Freytag modified the structure by adding two more points to the three-point structure. He created the five-point plot arc we use today (**FIGURE 1.3**). He saw common patterns in story arcs and created a diagram to illustrate that.

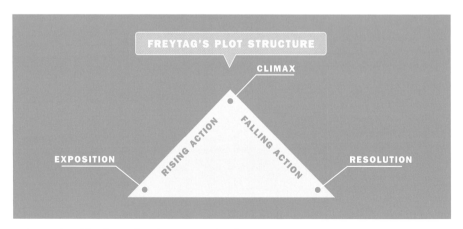

FIGURE 1.3 The five-point plot arc used today.

You can find other structures, such as a seven-point arc, as well. That one adds an *inciting incident* to the corner of the arc between the exposition and the rising action. It also adds what's called a *dénouement* after the resolution. These two plot points aren't necessarily absent from the current arc; they are more or less embedded in other plot points.

STORYTELLING AND EVOLUTION

Storytelling seems to be deeply engrained in the DNA of every person. Oral storytelling is as old as humanity. It was the very first form of communication along with visual storytelling in the form of cave paintings, pottery, and so on. Film brings those ancient techniques together very powerfully.

Why does it matter how long the story arc has been around? In a word: evolution. Without storytelling, how else would you explain how and where you were chased by a saber-toothed cat through the woods? Or that somebody ate this plant and got rid of an illness, but somebody else ate that one over there, which looks almost the same, and it made them sick? Humans pass on their important information through stories. The human mind has evolved with the story arc, and with stories in general, which remain an important part of our culture.

Our cultural traditions are all based on stories, and that includes religions. The Bible, for example, is a collection of stories. Regardless of your religious beliefs, you at least have to marvel at how the Bible is full of 2,000-year-old stories that still dictate the way some people live their lives, raise their children, and spend their Sunday mornings. That's beautiful. The Bible is an example of how powerful stories can be. In fact, every mythology and religion throughout history relies on storytelling.

MAXIMIZING THE INFLUENCE AND POTENTIAL OF STORIES

The influence of stories continues. To lower the intelligence scale several levels, consider the movie *The Fast and the Furious*. It's a movie about decking out cars with crazy after-market parts and then racing them. After the first of these movies came out, people flocked to stores that sold after-market car parts. They bought rims, tinted their windows, and installed new mufflers and brighter headlights and so forth due to the influence of the film.

Young people watched the movie and projected themselves into one character or the other, and the rest is history. When the movie ended, their personal story was just getting started. Kids in my high school who worked eight-dollar-an-hour jobs after school every day would spend three months' worth of pay on a new front bumper that made the car lower to the ground—all because they saw it in a movie.

When you tell a story, it's a good idea to be honest with yourself about the maximum possibility of influence or connection it can achieve—meaning, first identify the type of film you're making. Not everyone is making a film that's contending for an Oscar, or even being released in theaters.

If you're making a wedding film, for example, what's the maximum potential you can realistically achieve? Better yet, what's your goal? If you sell yourself short by just trying to get your clients to love it, then you haven't reached the maximum potential of a wedding film. Google "Stillmotion wedding film" and watch any one of their films. You might find yourself enjoying it. Why on earth would anyone enjoy someone else's wedding film? Because these films achieve the *maximum potential*. What does that mean? It means trying to make your film entertain a broad audience. If it's a wedding film, the couple you're making it for will most likely love just about anything. But if you can get a stranger to love it, you've succeeded.

If you're making an event film, the same rules apply. No one sat around in preproduction meetings for *The Fast and the Furious* and honestly thought they'd win Best Picture at the Oscars. They wanted a franchise. And they got one. They've made seven movies and sold billions in merchandise.

I'd say *The Fast and The Furious* achieved maximum potential. It's widely considered a bottom-tier film in the realm of cinema history, but its generational influence is unmatched. This means it burrowed its way into the minds of viewers. That's good storytelling, and when a story is well told, it means it was well edited. The pieces were given to you strategically. We know wedding films to be boring. If you can make someone care, even if for a moment, you've succeeded.

Think about the movie *Jaws*. Did you dare go to the beach after seeing the film? Did you go in the water? Did it feel the same to swim in the ocean? No, it didn't, I'll wager. Watch that film and focus on the presentation of the shots. Think about when the camera goes underwater, showing the legs of the swimmers. That could be you. Shots of the shark's fin approaching the shoreline? That could happen while you're there. The setting was *any old day at the beach*. What if that day was the day you happened to be there?

> **TIP** When you tell a story, ask yourself: How deep into the viewer's mind can I go?

Film is a visual medium. We have been communicating with visuals at least as long ago as we've been communicating with words. Think of cave paintings from 20,000 years ago. The artist used only the visual to communicate. *Visual* communication often enjoys a better universal understanding among people. If I say the word *happy*, it's not nearly as powerful as showing you a visual of a child with a smile stretching from ear to ear, looking at candy. The visual has more information, and it can include more detail in that information. The word *happy* is very vague. *How* happy? A little bit? A lot? Happy about what? A visual can answer those questions very easily.

Identifying with Characters

The last element of the story arc that needs to be understood before we break down the sections is exactly how people project themselves into a story. Every story has an arc and every scene has an arc (sometimes called a *flip*). Now I'm telling you that every important *character* in every story has an arc as well.

Characters/subjects are the portals to every story. They are the way you get viewers to buy into the story. The viewers identify with, relate to, and even empathize with the characters. In a way, they become the characters, or at least they compare themselves to the character.

The moment viewers make that personal connection, you own them. Think of a character arc as an entirely separate arc from the story you are telling. Obviously they overlap in a major way, but the character is special because it is the portal that gets viewers to buy into your story.

The character arc is a parallel running arc to the story. The difference is the character arc runs through several scenes or even the whole story. It feeds the big and little arcs of the story. In *The Pre-Nup*, each main character had an arc. Let's look at Philip Reed's:

1.   He has a fiancée who is a terrible person and treats him like garbage.

2.   Philip's fiancée takes her ring off and says she would put it back on for a million dollars.

3.   Philip comes home and finds out someone broke into his house. He also discovers he is the winner of 10 million dollars. His fiancée changes her tune to excited, nice, and loving.

4.   Philip kicks out the robber and the fiancée.

5.   Philip's life is great while his counterparts' lives are boring.

That's not the arc of the story, but the arc of Philip Reed. The points of Philip's character arc feed the points of the big story. The reason it's called a *flip* is because Philip's life was awful in the beginning and great by the end.

> **NOTE** Inside the main arc, many other arcs are going on at once. It's the editor's job to keep track of them all and assemble them in a way that takes advantage of all the climaxes, big or small, that are in the film.

The next section zooms in and explores the different parts of the story arc. Knowing where you are along the roller coaster is a big help in getting the viewers to participate in the story.

Exposition

Exposition is where every story begins. Notice back in Figure 1.1 that the exposition is a flat point in the arc. It's flat because not a lot of plot is happening yet. The exposition is where you give out crucial information to the viewer. For that reason, the exposition may be the most important part of the arc.

Your story is a world you created. The viewers need to know certain things in order to understand the events that will unfold in your story. Think about a film like *The Matrix*. You can't tell that story without first telling who the story is about and what the Matrix actually is. The exposition of that film doesn't end until Neo decides which pill to take. Everything that happens between the beginning and that point is the crucial information the viewers need to move on in the story.

Why Exposition Is So Important

This is not to say that the exposition isn't exciting. But in comparison to the rising action and the climax—which are packed with plot twists and story development, and the falling action and resolution that ride on the excitement of the plot points that came before—the exposition can feel uneventful.

So why is it so important? Because the exposition is when viewers decide whether they are in or out. They are given information such as who the characters are and where the story is taking place. (I break all this down for you in detail later in this section.) This information needs to be presented in a way that leads the viewers into the more exciting parts of the story without their becoming aware of the fact the story has transitioned into another phase. The exposition relies on the fact that viewers are *voluntarily* watching the film.

Going back to *The Pre-Nup* (Video 1.1), the assembly of the exposition keeps leading you. When you see the montage of the man breaking into the house and then the couple arguing, you don't really know it's their house that's being burgled. However, you have a pretty good idea. Most viewers will make that connection. They are participating. You were given just enough crucial information to draw your own conclusion about the conditions of the story. It doesn't matter whether the viewers are right or wrong about this—all that needs to happen is for a conclusion to be drawn.

It would be easy to remove the couple from the story until they come home. It's as simple as deleting a few scenes. The story would still make perfect sense. But then there wouldn't be enough information to lead the viewers across the arc. That could cause the viewers to give up or not connect with the story.

The plot arc is invisible to viewers. All they know is that what they're watching is either interesting or boring. But an editor must be constantly aware of the plot arc in order to determine what information can be released, and in what order it's released. Introducing the couple in the exposition of *The Pre-Nup* occurs for two major purposes:

- When the man is interrupted stealing the television, you think it's them. If you never saw them, you can't make that connection.
- When you first see them, you start to speculate about their integration into the story.

When these questions get answered, you're well into the action part of the story.

Remember that if you can't hook your viewers in the beginning, then it doesn't matter what happens later in the rising action or the other points in the arc, because the viewers will never make it that far. Filmmakers become obsessed with the ending—and that's a great philosophy—but if your ending doesn't satisfy the viewer, they can't unwatch what they've already seen. In the exposition, your job as the editor is to prepare viewers for the remainder of the story arc and get them excited for what is to follow.

Keeping in Mind What the Viewers Know at All Times

As you will see in Chapter 2, you should approach editing in a circular process rather than a linear approach. The circular process involves editing full cuts of scenes or full films and *then* making modifications, as opposed to making things perfect as you go.

You should be able to view a skeleton version of your story before constructing the beginning (see Chapter 2 for more on this). Knowing what the beginning feeds into is an important part of the storytelling process. Often editors become obsessed with the idea of editing a fantastic, mind-blowing, well-polished beginning before they construct the *narrative base*—a skeleton rough edit of your film that consists only of the narrative or the foundation of your film. (I discuss narrative base more in Chapter 3.) A big part of that desire comes from the logical starting point of the beginning in a linear approach to the editing process. But really it's because editors love the positive reinforcement of seeing a great beginning every time they watch their film during the editing process. That shows how important beginnings actually are—even the person creating the film craves it to lead them into other parts of the story. After all, an editor is also a viewer who longs for well-constructed stories.

When you construct your exposition, be very conscious of what information the viewers are seeing. One intangible skill of an editor is that they can keep the viewers in mind even while knowing a lot more information than the viewers know at any given moment. You must look at each part of the plot structure as a separate piece of the puzzle, all the while reminding yourself of the big picture. That means asking yourself questions and being honest and rigorous about the answers. For example, "What does the viewer know right now?" is a question to repeatedly ask yourself, because what you know and what the viewer knows are very different things.

You also don't want to tell them things they already know. That's a great way to bore your audience. I like to say, "Don't begin every film with the information that the sky is blue." The viewers already know a lot. They do live in the same world you do and see the same things. Movies have been around a very long time and they follow a certain structure that is a known quantity among the population (more on that in a moment). Viewers are smart. They can figure things out for themselves if you give them enough hints, and it's part of the fun for them to figure things out from your clues.

Viewers want a puzzle to solve. This is why a show like *Breaking Bad* can become a cultural phenomenon. Each season had a major reveal that required the viewers to constantly guess about how things would play out. We were always wrong, and we loved every second of it. Remember, it's important that the viewers are piecing things together on their own—whether they're right or wrong doesn't matter. On the other hand, if you beat them over the head with the information, you lose the puzzle and the allure of the unknown altogether.

Here's what any good exposition tries to accomplish:

1. Establish and introduce the characters.
2. Establish the setting.
3. Establish the mood and conditions that exists at the beginning.
4. Establish the characters' positions in the story.
5. Introduce the exciting force (conflict).

These five elements are included in the beginning of nearly every story. It's a lot of information to cover in a short period of time, so it's important to do it right—and quickly. The elements are listed in no particular order, with the exception of introducing the exciting force. That's the lead-in to the next plot point, so it should come at the end of the exposition.

Introducing the Characters

Let's begin with the characters. It's really hard to make a film about a bottle of water, or a pen, or a tissue. It's hard to make a film about any object. That's why almost any commercial about a product features people using the product, as opposed to just telling a story about the product itself. That's not because the producers were dying to spend extra money to pay actors. It's because people are essential to any story (and yes, commercials are stories, in their own way).

People are the most important element of any story. Characters are the portals in which the viewers transcend into the story. Viewers imagine themselves as the characters. That's why they become interested. Characters are the way you make your viewers a part of the action rather than passively observing what's happening in the film. You feel many different ways about the thousands of characters you've been introduced to over the course of your life watching films. You relate to or empathize with at least one particular character in each story. You like it when characters conduct themselves in a way that you would act in the particular situation. You know someone close to you who is exactly like a certain character you've been introduced to in films. You despise the actions of other characters and think they are evil. It matters less *how* you feel than it does that you *feel something*. If you feel something, you're a part of the story.

> *People are the most important element of any story.*

In the beginning, you need to introduce the main characters at the very least. Keep in mind the viewers should be drawing their own conclusions. In expositions, you'll find a lot of silent shots focusing on a character that's being developed. For example, in *The Pre-Nup* I held on the shot of the robber after he broke into the house. He gave a creepy smile. I didn't have to include that shot. The story has been told. He's inside the house. But letting the viewers see him for a solid six seconds, revealing his reaction and thoughts and emotions, helps develop his character. Editing choices like that help develop characters.

It's not the fact that the robber smiled. It's the timing of the smile, the lighting in the room, the music selection, the camera movement, the context of the story, the fact you don't know him or trust him—all of this combines to influence your perception of this character. This is why being aware of storytelling overall matters. That smirk from the robber has a ripple effect. It's more than an expression—it's affected by and affects everything around it.

Keep in mind that you'll spend the entire film developing your characters, so don't give everything away right up front. By the end of the exposition, the audience should have a firm understanding of the main characters' personalities and general outlook on life. Why? Because, as I mention earlier, every story is a collaboration between filmmaker and viewer. The filmmaker poses a set of conditions, and viewers process those and then ask themselves questions. Like when there is a knock at the door in *The Pre-Nup*, you ask yourself, "Who's that?"

The filmmaker then answers the viewers' questions with more conditions. The question is "Who's at the door?" Then I show who's at the door. By introducing new characters and an element to the story (10 million dollars), I've introduced new conditions. I've answered the question of "Who's at the door?," and now the viewers know that I, the storyteller, will answer the questions they have.

It's important to note that I answered that question with a new set of conditions. Publishers Clearing House is there with 10 million dollars for Philip Reed. The burglar is not Philip Reed, but he pretends to be.

Once that happens, the viewers then help the filmmaker justify the existence of these conditions. This means that the actions that will follow make sense inside the conditions that are currently laid out in the film. At some point, the viewers will jump the gun in their minds by saying to themselves, "Oh, I get it. The couple live there, and they are about to come home." Now the viewers help create anticipation with that prediction, and by predicting the future, they are accepting what has already happened. Knowing that as an editor is absolutely crucial. This is where rhythm comes into play (*rhythm* is explored in Chapter 5). For this example, all you need to know is that, as the editor, you have to leave time in the scene to allow the viewers to go through this mental process, all without slowing down the film. Then the film keeps going.

The robber invites the sweepstakes crew inside, and he needs to keep the lie alive in order to not get caught.

A character is dropped into the conditions the story has laid out and behaves in a certain way. The character's behavior should make sense and be justifiable. An editor does that by making sure the character is correctly developed in the beginning, which then sets up his or her behavior later on as things change. The story conditions do change and so do characters through the story.

Every character has an arc, remember? Great characters are different by the end of the story because of the journey they've completed. But the journey doesn't happen in the exposition.

▶ CHARACTER ARC IN ACTION

If Harry is a shy, nerdy boy who's a homebody, then having him walk up to an attractive woman in a bar and ask for her number makes no sense. But if a series of events in the story gradually bring him to that bar, and the story has taught him lessons and prepared him a little, and somehow he finds the courage to approach the woman—then that's your plot arc (also known as a flip).

Here is how that complete arc might play out:

1. Harry is a shy nerdy boy hanging out with his cool older brother. His older brother is explaining to him how to pick up girls.

2. Harry gets invited to the bar by his friends.

3. While at the bar, Harry recites what his brother told him, but pretends it's his words. He pretends to be cool. His friends challenge him to talk to a girl at the bar and get her number. After some hesitation or resistance, Harry approaches the girl and sits down. The hesitation helps maintain his character. This falls into the hands of the writer, but also the editor. It might mean holding on to a shot that shows his hesitation longer than normal. What is normal? Chapter 4 talks about pacing.

4. He ends up getting her number.

5. Harry is not a shy nerd anymore—now he is cool and may be on his way to having a girlfriend.

Notice how Harry started the story as a nerd and ended up cool. That's a complete flip. But you can't develop him as a nerd who suddenly gets a woman's number all in the exposition. Such a change has to come later in the arc.

Establishing the Characters' Positions in the Story

Introducing multiple characters is common in beginnings. The more characters, the more portals for the viewers. But the more characters, the more time it takes to develop them. Keep that in mind when thinking about ideas for a story. It can help you decide which characters to focus on when constructing it. If you have multiple characters, you'll need to establish their positions in the story—meaning where they are in the grand scheme of the story. Character A is a poor man who lives on a street corner, and character B is a rich stockbroker who lives in the penthouse of a nice apartment building. Their *positions* are their conditions. In the exposition, it's very important that you hold off on connecting these characters. Let the audience do that for you.

Remember, audiences love to make connections on their own. We've all seen enough movies to know that if we're watching a homeless man live on the street and a rich man going about his day living in the penthouse suite, somehow they'll connect. The viewers already know that—let them predict how. If the viewers start working on connecting these characters, that means they are participating in the process. Boom! You own them. Whether they are right or wrong about their predictions is irrelevant in the equation. All that matters is they are playing the game. At some point, you'll connect the characters in the story—but not yet.

Establishing the Setting

The *setting* of a story is more than just where a story takes place. The setting is all the details of that world. The idea is to give the viewers a sense of where they are. I don't mean just in terms of geographical location—I mean the type of location. You're setting could be Anytown, U.S.A., as many stories are. But what type of town is it? Is it a safe town? Is it highly populated or deserted? What type of social class is part of the town? Is it beautiful, wide open country, or loud and crammed by cars and people? You have to decide what shots best explain the setting to the viewers and help them do some of the work for you as far as imagining the setting.

In other words, you need more than just a shot of New York City. You need a shot of the street. You need some shots of the corner, some people walking by, dogs barking, police cars speeding away. Paint the picture. The more the viewers can imagine the setting, the more real it's going to feel. A great example of this is the show *The Walking Dead*. The very first scene of the pilot episode that comes before the credit sequence has nothing to do with the actual story. It's only there to illustrate the zombie apocalypse.

They didn't just drop me into the story without showing me what world I'm in. The setting is your universe. You need to begin by showing the viewers around a little bit.

That doesn't mean the story can never change locations. It means you need to establish the setting so that when it changes, the viewers understand there has been a change in setting. The importance of setting in film is often forgotten because these city shots, or establishing the setting, can be generic. Including lots of detailed shots to paint the picture, however, is a great way to draw the viewers in. It goes back to having the viewers connect the dots. What if I start a film with a sequence of shots that go in this order:

- Bag going on a conveyer belt
- Someone removing shoes
- Shot of a computer screen showing X-ray images of bags

Where are we? A recent airport security line, of course. Build your scene from details. Then reward the viewers by showing a wider shot that confirms this is airport security. Give the viewers a chance to imagine their own airport before you show them yours.

Remember, you are creating a world that's not real, so you have to make it feel real. Whether your film is based on reality or fiction, it's still a two-dimensional flat world that someone is watching on a screen. Three of the five senses are eliminated. Sensory deprivation is a fascinating concept. When a person climbs inside a dark water tank, removing all senses from the equation, often they start to hallucinate. The mind is trying to compensate for the lack of the senses by filling in the blanks—proving that the mind is hardwired to fill in the blanks for what it doesn't know. If viewers don't know something, their brain should be trying to figure it out.

Establishing Mood

Of course, with a film the senses aren't really eliminated. What's eliminated is the filmmaker's ability to use three of the senses in creating another reality. You have sight and sound—that's it. That's why including details about the setting is so important to the exposition. The viewers must be able to use what you provide to fill in the blanks. Ask yourself, "How do I want my viewers to feel?" If you want them to feel cold, show shots of snow, people exhaling vapor, people wearing jackets and gloves. That kind of detail helps viewers project themselves into the environment you're trying to create. Weather, time of year, time of day, specific place, street names, house numbers, social class—these are all details that help the viewers create the rest of the world for you.

Be strategic in the fact that each shot you show helps the viewers create in their mind the setting you're trying to create. Remember, you start with nothing. You must construct the film's world, and each shot provides information viewers will process when they see it. A shot of a red leaf blowing across the screen is pretty, but it also tells us much more than the action we're witnessing. That leaf tells us that it's fall, it's breezy outside. With one shot you can tell the viewers what time of year it is and let them estimate the temperature outside. If next comes a wide shot showing a park with people walking and wearing jackets, that confirms our prediction of the season and the weather. Each shot leads into another. Setting feeds into mood. Is your story dark and twisted, bright and happy, or somewhere in the middle? You can use setting details to set the tone.

Establishing the Conditions and Conflict

What are the conditions of the story? Let's say Brandon has trouble paying attention in school, and it's putting his desire, and his father's desire, for him to go to an Ivy League school in jeopardy. Those are conditions. It's important that the viewers know those conditions because they will be different by the end of the story. The point isn't to just see that the conditions change, but to see how the conditions change. Part of those conditions is something called the *exciting force* or *conflict*.

Conflict is the driving force of every story. It is what your characters are trying to overcome. Conflict is present in all plot points. If you are telling a story, you have at least one of the six types of conflicts (see Chapter 2 for the breakdown of the six conflicts). For example, the conflict in *The Pre-Nup* would be the real Philip Reed trying to prove who he is and getting that burglar out of his house so he can keep his money—otherwise known as human versus human, or relational conflict.

You'll explore the six types of conflict in Chapter 2, but let's quickly add one to Brandon's story. Brandon has a heavy case of attention deficit disorder, and his family doesn't have health insurance because his father recently lost his job. That's a conflict. It's not that the viewers want to see Brandon get into college. The viewers want to see *how* he and his family overcome the challenges laid out in the conditions you create in the beginning.

Once you lay out all the elements, your exposition is complete, and it's time to move on to the rising action.

Rising Action

If you've done your exposition correctly and efficiently, and your viewers are still watching, congratulations! As I've mentioned, the beginning is the part of the arc the viewers need in order to understand the rest of the story. If you show up late to a movie theater and miss the first 10 minutes of a film, chances are you've missed a lot. The rising action depends on those initial conditions you set up. In terms of the act structure, the rising action starts off Act 2.

The rising action is just what it sounds like. It's all about building intensity and anticipation. Back to the roller coaster—imagine you've just pulled away from the loading bay. The ride is moving slowly and the track is flat. You have a decent view of the rest of the ride. The second the roller coaster starts up the first hill, you begin the rising action.

Remember this and remember it well: It's all about anticipation. It's a combination of the conditions you've presented, the characters you've placed in those conditions, and the viewers' participation. Referring back to *The Pre-Nup*, the exposition ends and the rising action begins at the end of the first scene with the couple. Now you know who the story is about and you are creating the obvious anticipation in your head. *This guy broke into a house and the people are going to come home and find him.* But not so fast, because the story is about to take a turn when there is a knock at the door. The viewers think they know who it is, and as long as they are thinking, you've done your job correctly.

If the viewers are piecing together a bit of information in the exposition, or guessing how things will connect, it enhances the anticipatory feeling when they enter the rising action. The only thinking or piecing together that should occur in the rising action is the anticipation of how the conditions will come together. If the viewers are given nothing to gain their participation in the exposition, then reeling them into the rising action will be much harder. The progression of the viewers' mind is just as important as the progression of the story arc. After all, the viewer's experience is what you're really trying to control. The good news is that if the beginning is well constructed, the rising action is fairly easy to construct.

Here is what the rising action must do:

1. Develop and establish the conflict.
2. Connect the characters and the conflicts (if you haven't already done so).
3. Build anticipation.
4. Give a clear path to the climax.

Unlike the exposition's list of goals, the rising action's list is in order of priority. No, there isn't a strict rulebook for what to do and what order to do it in. This is just a basic, common, suggested structure.

Developing the Conflict

The last thing the exposition does is introduce the exciting force or conflict. And the first thing you'll want to do in the rising action is zero in on developing that conflict. The rising action should start with some sort of connection back to the conditions you set in the exposition.

Coming back to *The Pre-Nup* and focusing on the burglar: It's safe to assume he's not rich. This is information we have in the beginning. It's also safe to assume the owner of the house is not well off either. Then comes the rising action, and millions of dollars are introduced into the story. Viewers immediately understand: Every character is going to want that money.

When you move into the rising action, it's important to note the editing decisions that affect the storytelling. After the idea of the 10 million dollars is introduced, the film cuts to a scene of the couple in the car and she talks about not putting the ring on for a million dollars. That was an editing choice—to make those moments happen one after the other. It was not scripted, nor was it filmed that way.

Be careful to not repeat your development of the exposition. Move forward. Your job now is to show the viewers why they needed all the information provided in the beginning. Let them use that information to start piecing the story together. The viewers are internally processing everything you've given them so far.

The overall goal of the rising action is to build toward an eventual climax, both in the story and in the viewer's mind. For example, suppose I establish that Jenny is poor, Tommy is rich, and they are both in a convenience store at the same time. Rich Tommy buys a lottery ticket with a hundred dollar bill, and poor Jenny counts out nickels to buy a small bottle of water. Jenny and Tommy smile at each other and have quick conversation that ends with Tommy buying Jenny the water. Then they leave and go their separate ways.

Jenny comes home to find out she's evicted. That would end the exposition because we've learned all the points we need to get started. We know who the story is about, the setting, their positions in the story, the mood, and the exciting force. The exciting force is Jenny being evicted. The first thing I'd want to do in the rising action would be to build on Jenny's struggles. As an editor, I may choose to go complex and construct a series of shots of Jenny getting into credit card debt or working hard jobs for small

pay. Or I may choose to save time and hold on a shot of Jenny looking at an electric bill. I show the bill, then I show Jenny's face. Here is a little editing trick: The viewers see what you want them to see, and they see what's in the context of the story. If I show Jenny smiling at an electric bill in the context of this story, the viewers will see it as a smile of frustration.

Whatever way you decide to establish Jenny's struggles, just know that the viewers remember that lottery ticket Tommy bought right in front of her face.

Building on Jenny's struggles should feel like a seamless continuation of the beginning, but we have actually entered into the rising action part of the story. The viewers don't need more information about the conditions now. The viewers are now living in the conditions with the main characters and should be wondering how Jenny will resolve this problem.

Once you've begun developing the conflict, it's time for the story to move into the character connection and conflict connection phase.

Connecting Characters and Conflicts

Connecting the characters is important. Of course, in stories most characters connect. The viewers know that. They don't need to see Jenny and Tommy literally run into each other at the convenience store in the exposition to know the characters are connected or will connect at some point. You can show them separately, like the burglar and the couple in *The Pre-Nup*. The question now is *how* they will connect.

In this story, the next thing to do is build on that connection. Maybe Jenny and Tommy are connected in a much deeper way. Let's say the next part of the rising action shows Tommy at his father's house, and he finds a photograph of a young girl that looks exactly like Jenny. You can illustrate the importance of this photo and the connection of the characters by how long you show the photo. Or if you show the photo at all. Showing Tommy's reaction to the photo might make the viewers identify with Tommy, but showing the photo first and making Tommy's reaction secondary could draw you to the *connection* more than the *reaction*. It would depend on how you want your viewers to feel, or what you want them to take away from the scene. Maybe Tommy isn't a hundred percent sure the picture is of Jenny, but he's pretty sure it is her from when she was young. The viewers are going to ask the same thing as Tommy: "Why is there a photograph of this girl in his father's house?"

Each time you open a door in a story, a new door is waiting behind it. You know in the beginning of the story that these two characters are connected. You walk through

that door only to find out things go much deeper than you thought. Tommy's father has a photo of her. What are the odds? And how did this happen?

The more doors you open, the more you want to open the next one. Anticipation builds on anticipation. Be careful, though—there are limits. You don't want to be opening doors without closing a few. This is where gaining credibility as a storyteller does matter. The viewers need to trust that you will answer certain questions.

The next goal of the rising action is to build anticipation.

Building Anticipation

You don't do anything specific to build anticipation except keep doing what you're doing. In other words, there's no specific section of the rising action in which to build anticipation. The whole thing should build anticipation. This can mean holding out on your smaller reveals for longer.

For example, when Tommy sees the picture of Jenny, maybe you show his face and his reaction first. Maybe you hold on that a few seconds longer than you normally would. Let's say the normal duration for a reaction shot is four seconds, and you decide to hold it for seven seconds. You can get away with this in the rising action because the viewers are in an anticipatory mindset. Time will feel shorter. During the climax, your shots tend to be quicker (I explore pacing at length in Chapter 4).

Leading to the Climax

Now, just before you get to the top of the roller coaster, something needs to happen. Lead your viewers to the eventual climax. When the viewers are at the top of the roller coaster, they should know it. Maybe Tommy is sitting home that night watching television, thinking about the weird connection with Jenny, and he finds out from the television that he won the lottery. That is what's called a *plot twist*—a plot twist that instantly puts us in a climactic state. A plot twist isn't a prerequisite to the climax, but if your story has one, it usually happens somewhere between the climax and the ending. A plot twist is when the story takes an unexpected turn. It can feel like a climax to the viewers no matter where it happens. As an editor, you'd treat these moments as a climax.

Not every story needs to have a plot twist, but when they do, plot twists tend to come at the end of the rising and/or the falling action (covered later in this chapter). The viewers can now start to predict how the film will resolve. If you draw enough

attention to the lottery ticket and the element of money, it seems logical that Jenny could end up with the money.

The storyteller doesn't *move* the viewers in the climax—the viewers move themselves. All the viewers need to do is have a clear path to the climax, and the clear path to the climax is set up by the filmmaker. When Tommy wins the lottery, it's natural for a viewer to think, "He's going to give Jenny some of that money." The viewers anticipate a logical climax. This thought is what takes us into the climax because we soon find out the answer to the biggest question in the story. It's a storyteller's responsibility to set this up, but as always it's your job as the editor to draw attention to this moment. The solution could be as simple as the ordering of shots (explored in Chapter 4).

It's easily understood that Tommy being rich and winning the lottery will connect with Jenny and the photograph. The viewers know that much based on the conditions you've presented and the built-in story arc knowledge they have because they've seen plenty of films and read many stories.

Now the roller coaster has hit the peak of the ride and you're ready to drop and enter into the climax of the film.

Climax

The climax might be the most misunderstood plot point of the story structure. The big misconception might be in the word *climax* itself. Simply put, the climax is just the turning point of the story. Most of its intensity comes from the buildup of the rising action and the conditions presented in the exposition. In other words, the climax will almost form itself if you've constructed the beginning and rising action correctly.

Although the climax may be the most misunderstood plot point, it's the easiest to construct. The climax is in fact the *point* of your story. The climax of the final episode of *Breaking Bad* (spoiler alert) is when the gun starts going off from Walt's popped trunk. But it would mean nothing without the whole scene of Walt almost getting killed by Jack or losing his car keys.

If your climax struggles to retain viewers or extract emotion, then chances are your problem lies in the previous plot points. The major difference between the climax and the rest of the film is that the pacing is different in the climax. It's constructed in its own unique way.

> **NOTE** *The climax is the point of your story, but it's the plot points leading up to it that make it the climax.*

This Is Your Brain on Climax

This is not a book on science, but it's important to understand the role science plays in the storytelling process. After all, the brain is what you're trying to manipulate when you tell a story. If you understand how the viewer's brain works, and when it's at its most active state, you can control the length of shots by understanding when the viewers are the most engaged.

The rising action is a buildup to the climax—the ride up the roller coaster. As we experience on the roller coaster, it's the very second before you drop that is the most climactic moment. Yes, the drop down is the thrilling part. Yes, the drop down is where the people on the ride scream. Yes, the drop down is the point of riding the roller coaster—as the climax is the point of a story. But the reason it's the most exciting part, and the reason people scream on the way down, is because of what happens in the brain *before* you drop. The climax isn't just the very top of the arc—it lasts for a good portion of the drop—but the absolute unquestioned moment of extreme intensity that happens in the second before the drop. Understanding why is to understand a simple brain function. There is a part of the brain called the nucleus accumbens. This part of the brain receives a dose of dopamine and is associated with pleasure, excitement, and anticipation. Those are the three words that matter here.

Here's another way of thinking about the climax. Let's say you love cheeseburgers. Now you're driving along the highway on a road trip and the craving pops into your brain, "I really want a cheeseburger." A small dose of dopamine is pumped into the nucleus accumbens. This is your brain "rewarding itself." It turns out there's a great burger place just 15 miles away, so you decide to make a detour to satisfy the craving. With every mile closer, the reward system pumps more dopamine into the brain—more and more and more until you finally sit down and order this highly anticipated cheeseburger.

Here's where it gets tricky. You might think that the first bite of the burger is the climax, but it's not. It's the second right *before* the burger hits your lips for the very first time. That is when the reward system in your brain is wildly out of control, pumping dopamine faster than you might imagine. Once you take that bite, though, it's all downhill from there. The most climactic moment is the second *before* you take that first bite. The climax might actually last as long as it takes to finish the burger, but the *peak* is the very second before the first bite.

That little lesson in neuroscience wasn't meant to bore you but to teach you a very important lesson: It's all about the anticipation. The more the viewers *anticipate* the climax, the more the reward system will pump dopamine, and the better your story will be. This same brain function occurs while watching movies. The difference with

movies is that it's up to the storyteller to build enough anticipation so that the viewers crave "the burger."

What's really interesting about this is that this brain function is a one-time deal. After you've experienced something for the very first time, the brain function you experience every time after that, while doing the same thing, is a simulation of that initial brain function. Imagine watching the most intense movie ever for the second time. The experience isn't the same. This means you have one chance to get the viewers to experience a climatic state from watching your film. The climax is one of the only areas of the film where drawing things out, within reason, can work in your favor.

> **NOTE** This reaction to repeated exposure to the climax occurs to everyone—with the exception of addicts. That's where this brain study comes from. They found that if you're addicted to something, each time you go through that same experience, your brain thinks it's happening for the very first time.

Goals of the Climax

Here's what a good climax must do:

1. Capitalize on the most intense moment of the story.
2. Connect back to the beginning. The climax is based on the original conditions you presented from the start.
3. Turn the corner.

I already touched on capitalizing on the most intense moment of the story from a psychological standpoint. From the perspective of editing, the climax is when you want the pacing to be its fastest while at the same time understanding the exact moment to hold a shot (more about pacing in Chapter 4).

CAPITALIZING ON THE INTENSE MOMENT

Imagine a simple footrace among five characters. Benny has been established in the beginning of the story as the main character and the underdog. The race starts and the runners take off. Benny's dead last. You'd want to build intensity with the rising action. You'd show a shot of Benny's feet picking up speed and then a wide shot showing he's gaining ground. The cuts would get faster as the story developed and we moved up the plot arc. (That's not always the case, but in this particular case it is.)

When you move into the climax, you could capitalize on the emotion by cutting to an extreme close-up shot of Benny's face, particularly focusing on his eyes closing while running, possibly in slow motion. Focusing so close on his eyes and the fact they are closed helps you take on the perspective of the character as he drowns out everything around him. You'd do the same thing as the viewer, because that's all you can see. Fading down the background noise would amplify things even more. (Audio is explored in Chapter 7.) You could also show beads of sweat coming down his brow. The sound of the crowd could be louder, cheering, "Benny, Benny, Benny." Holding that close-up shot of his face, at the particular time, accomplishes two goals:

- It's close enough to have us zero in on the emotion.
- By removing the context of the actual racing, it forces the viewer's brain into a state of anticipation. "Did he pass them?" "Is it over?"

The longer you hold on that shot, the more the viewers remain in the moment just before the metaphorical burger hits their lips.

Holding on a shot has limits. You can't do it forever, of course, but a few seconds is perfectly acceptable. The duration of shots, and shot selection (discussed in Chapter 4) are ways of capitalizing on the most intense moment of the story.

CONNECTING BACK TO THE BEGINNING

Connecting back the beginning is a must during the climax. Show the viewers why they needed to know certain elements of the story in the beginning. The climax is where you start connecting all that stuff you included in the exposition.

> **TIP** Anton Chekhov, the Russian dramatist and short story writer, stated his principle that if you show a gun in chapter 1, it had better fire a shot by chapter 3. Everything in your exposition should be there for a reason. Don't show something that has no purpose in the story. Don't introduce a plot point that doesn't come back later in the story.

To use the gun reference again, let's look at the finale to *Breaking Bad*. In the exposition of the episode, Walt is at a diner and buys a very ridiculous gun that we know he's not physically able to operate in his condition. Now, if that gun is never going to be fired, why would we watch him buy it? Everything needs to have a purpose. Of course, it fires many shots at the end of the climax, and Walt is not physically operating it.

As the editor, you can make the viewers remember things based on shot selection (Chapter 2) and shot duration (Chapter 4). This is an important skill for an editor

because it helps to tell the story through visuals. The editor has a good amount of control about what the viewers pay attention to, what they remember, and what they may gloss over and forget. I discuss all this in Chapter 2.

TURNING THE CORNER

Don't let the ride get stuck on the best part. You must lead the viewers into the final chapter of the story.

Once the climax has been revealed, the film is no longer about anticipation. Now it's all about the falling action and the resolution. These are the wind-down parts of the plot arc. It's called *turning the corner*.

I've often heard people express their desire to see films end on a high note. If you're making a film that will be an opener to an event, or a video that plays before a basketball game on the Jumbotron, then ending on a high note is the right move because your film is only part of a bigger story.

If you're telling a complete standalone story, though, never end on a high note. It's the cardinal sin of storytelling and editing. By "ending on a high note," I mean ending a story at the most intense moment. This doesn't refer to a state of emotion. It means don't end a film when you've reached maximum intensity. Ride that wave all the way back down almost to where you started.

Ending on a high note is like leaving the roller coaster before the ride is over—a bad idea. Think of the exposition and the rising action as the legwork you put in to create the climax and make it feel like a climax. The falling action and resolution are where you reap the rewards, and the viewers reap the rewards for the time they've invested. This is why the falling action can almost feel like it's a second climax, because it follows directly after the climax.

I keep using the final episode of *Breaking Bad* as an example because, as far as an arc is concerned, it's executed flawlessly. When the climax is completed, after Walt's makeshift machine gun goes off and eliminates everyone inside the house, viewers are on a high of intensity. I was standing up with my hands on my head. Did they end it there? Of course not. That intensity is going to last for a little while no matter what comes on the screen next. Even if there was a commercial break I'd still be wired. If you watch this episode, or think back to your memory of it, you'll remember a moment of silence after the gun stops firing. That's for audience digestion, known as rhythm, and it's executed perfectly (see Chapter 5 for more). After the filmmakers allow us time to digest, Jesse (the other main character) settles a score with the only bad guy left alive. That's a really intense moment. But if you just watched that scene by itself, it wouldn't have nearly the same impact. That's because the viewers are still remembering the intensity of the climax. Jesse settling this score is part of what's known as the *falling action*.

Falling Action

The climax is the most tense or intense moment of the story, but it's not the end of the action. When you enter the falling action, that means the feeling of anticipation is gone. Anticipation is one of those things an audience lives for, but it's not the only thing. The falling action (the closing part of Act 2) can still be a great part of the story.

The falling action has only two goals:

- Ride on the intensity of the climax
- Lead the viewers into the resolution.

An example of a falling action would be when Philip Reed kicks his fiancée out of the house in *The Pre-Nup*. It's not really a part of the climax, but it is part of the action of the story. The real story was between Philip Reed and the burglar.

The falling action is all about leading the viewers into the resolution, while at the same time riding the initial intensity of the climax. The falling action is a unique part of the plot structure in that it has one characteristic the other plot points do not possess: The falling action can be bridged with the climax to add extra intensity. Filmmakers do this all the time to give the viewers an extended climax.

When constructing your story on the editing board (the timeline, as referenced in Chapter 6), you may choose to take the falling action, a separate part of the arc, and combine it with the climax to create a climax that "feels longer." When doing this, you haven't changed anything about the plot arc. The way you do it is by *not* creating separation after the climax and maintaining the climactic pace. This has to do with rhythm, explored in Chapter 5.

In *The Pre-Nup,* after Philip Reed kicks everyone out of the house, there is a very short fade to black before the next scene. That is one of many examples of separation. It gives the audience time to digest, even if it's just for a second. If you wanted to maintain intensity, though, you would not create separation. When you create separation, the intensity starts building all over again. This is a good technique to use in shorter films that run under 15 minutes.

When the falling action has concluded, your viewers should have a clear understanding that the film is going to end every soon. They should also have an idea how it will end. *Soon* is a relative term based on the length of your film. In a two-hour feature film, *soon* could mean ending in the next 10 to 15 minutes. In a 10-minute film, *soon* could mean 30 to 45 seconds.

Whatever the case may be, the viewers need that clear path to the ending. That can come from the viewers knowing that story elements are wrapping up or in the story separation (discussed in Chapter 5). For now, an example would be the simple dip to black that happens in *The Pre-Nup* after Philip Reed kicks everyone out of the house.

> **NOTE** *The falling action is a mirror version of the rising action. The difference is that the rising action leads into the climax, and the falling action leads into the resolution.*

Resolution

Welcome to the most dangerous part of the plot structure and Act 3: the resolution or ending.

Why Endings Are Hard

Think about every television series you've seen all the way through, and how each ended. The majority of TV series do not end well—by which I mean they do not satisfy the viewers. That's not because people don't understand how to end stories. Unsatisfactory endings to televisions series happen for two reasons:

- It's difficult to satisfy the public's desire for certain plot points.
- If your story is good, the audience is usually bitter about it being over.

No ending will eliminate the pain of the story concluding for the viewer. This is just the nature of endings. This is one reason why leading the viewers into the resolution during the falling action is imperative. Viewers need time to prepare for the fact that it's almost over. In a nutshell, you're working against the grain.

The resolution is your most vulnerable time as a storyteller. It's easy to do more damage than good. The key here is to make it short, sweet, and to the point. In the other plot points, I gave you a list of what you should be doing. For the resolution, I'll start with two things to *not* do.

DO NOT INTRODUCE NEW CHARACTERS

It is extremely important to not introduce new characters at the end. Introducing a new character at this point makes the viewers feel like the story is not over. It goes against everything the falling action should do. At this point in the story, your viewers should be attached to the characters they've been with during the entire ride. Introducing a new character would require a great deal of character development, and this is something you don't have time for. Instead, you need to conclude the stories of the characters you've already established. Show shots of them that have a concluding feel:

- Shots of main characters walking away from the camera. Walking away feels final, whereas a shot of them walking toward the camera feels inviting and new.

- Shots that fade to black. I discuss this in Chapter 5 with regard to rhythm.

- When a character is exiting the film for the final time, have them use words that suggest they are leaving the story, such as "goodbye" or "see you soon."

- Shots from a rising camera indicate that you're leaving the scene.

DO NOT INTRODUCE NEW PLOT POINTS

Introducing new plot points at the end is the cardinal mistake of resolutions. A new plot point is an irrelevant story that distracts from the overall goal of the story. It's like getting the dessert menu after a nice dinner to find a list of great ice cream, cakes, coffee, and a piece of fried chicken. You'd look at that menu and think to yourself, "fried chicken?" Sure, it gets the viewers to ask questions, but this is not the time for questions, this is the time for answers. You wouldn't order the chicken, obviously, but you would be distracted by its very existence. You need to focus on the ending, not new beginnings.

Tying Up Loose Ends

The only requirement of the resolution is to tie up the loose ends. Tying up loose ends is actually the job of a scriptwriter, but you need to complement the process with good shot selection (more on this in Chapter 2).

Any questions the viewers may have asked themselves in the exposition need to be answered here and now. Tying up loose ends in a film is also called *putting a bow on the story*. Not everything needs to be tied up, but the major story arcs need to resolve themselves. That's the important characteristic of the resolution. Leaving things open-ended is a mistake for any major plot point. In *Fight Club*, we finally got to see what Project Mayhem's main mission is. In *The Matrix,* Neo finally becomes *The One.* If those things never happened, why would we watch the movie?

As for smaller story points, putting a bow on them is optional. These are called the *aha moments* of the resolution. It's a story arc that completes itself even though it's not required to achieve a resolution. A perfect example is how the burglar ended up with the fiancée in *The Pre-Nup.* I didn't need to show that at all to end the story. But it was a small plot arc that developed through the film, and I think it makes a good, funny, lasting impression on the viewer. The order in which the shots are presented feeds this concept directly (I discuss the order of shots in Chapter 5). The more of these little holes that close themselves in the end, the more satisfied your viewers will be.

ALWAYS REMEMBER THE STORY ARC

The thing to keep in mind about the story arc and how it relates to editing is this: Ask yourself, "Where am I in the arc?" You need to know the answer in order to know when the viewers need to be fed certain information. Giving the viewers information at the wrong time is a mistake. Understanding the elements of the plot arc is critical because it's the foundation for all your decision making. And shot selection, the order of shots, the pacing, the rhythm—all of the concepts that are in the chapters to follow are about making choices.

When you're deciding what shot to choose, there will be many right and wrong answers. Some right answers will work better than others. You'll never be able to definitively say, "This is the only shot that belongs here," or "This is the right pace for this scene," but you'll always be able to answer the question, "Where am I in the plot arc?" Knowing that answer is the first step in the right direction.

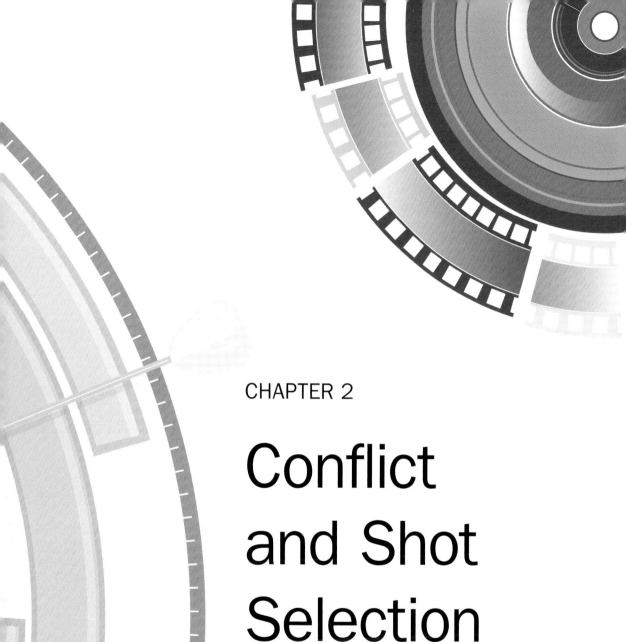

CHAPTER 2

Conflict and Shot Selection

Good editing comes down to decision making. Now that you understand the story arc, as discussed in Chapter 1, you have some foundation on which to base your decisions. Making the right choices when you're editing can be the difference between polished editing and choppy editing.

Shot selection comes into play in a very big way when it comes to conflict. Chapter 1 briefly touches on conflict, sometimes known as the exciting force. Conflict is what your main character is trying to overcome in the story. In storytelling, there are six types of conflicts you can center your story around, and I cover them all in this chapter. Although conflict is more of a writing or storytelling concept, like the story arc, it's important to understand the six types of conflicts, the rules of conflict, and how shot selection is directly influenced by the presence of conflict in the story. Before getting into shot selection, this chapter explores the conflicts possible within the story.

Shot selection should reinforce the conflict that already exists in your story.

When I'm editing any film and deciding what shot should I cut to next, I always ask myself, "What's the conflict?" Shot selection should reinforce the conflict that already exists in your story. The editor does not create the conflict; the editor draws attention to and highlights the conflict in the subtlest of ways.

Shot selection is one of the primary decisions you'll make during editing—and it's one of the most important concepts to understand when learning to be a great editor. Nothing random happens when it comes to shot selection. As with everything, it's all about the end game and the psychological effect on the viewer. The great thing about shot selection, when it comes to editing, is that it can teach you what type of shots you'll end up needing to set yourself up for success during editing.

If you're new to filmmaking and plan to start out as an editor, or you're thinking about adding cinematography to your arsenal of skills, editing will prime your mind for the type of shots you want and how many shots you need. In a scripted environment, it's straightforward because things are planned before the shoot. An *unscripted* environment, on the other hand, can leave your hands tied in the editing room because the pace of filming is faster and shots are forgotten in the filming process.

First, let's explore what exactly conflict is in filmmaking.

The Six Types of Conflict

What is conflict? Conflict is the dramatic struggle between two forces in the story. Conflict is present in every story—always. This is an undisputed, nondebatable concept. Within a story, six types of conflict can be present. Before delving into the types, however, I'll cover a few rules about conflict.

You *can* have a film without conflict, but it would not be a story. You must have two driving forces in a story to even have a plot. If you're making corporate films, wedding films, or other similar films, the key is to not always associate conflict with negativity. All identifying *conflict* means is identifying the two driving forces in the story.

No conflict, no plot. I'm not saying every video must have conflict. However, every *story* must have a conflict. Maybe the video you're making is not intended to be a story with a structure or a plot. In that case, conflict may or may not be present in the story. Maybe you're making an infomercial, and it's just a clip of a man talking to the camera about the latest weight-loss pill. Sure, maybe no conflict exists (although that would fall under social conflict, as discussed later in this chapter). The point here is that if you're making videos like that, then you're doing just that—making videos. Storytelling, by contrast, is all about conflict. Everything explored in this book is here to enhance the story and the viewer's experience of that story. The bottom line is that if you want to have a plot, you must have conflict.

The bottom line is that if you want to have a plot, you must have conflict.

How do you determine what the conflict is? The good news here is that your judgment is not on trial here. This means that what *you* perceive to be conflict in the story is irrelevant. It's all about the main character's perception of the conflict. That is the deciding factor in pinpointing the conflict present in a plot. If you and I watch a film, we might perceive the conflict differently. So, whom should the editor cater to? Neither. The main character is the means to determining the conflict. If someone walks up to a main character in the story and says, "The world is going to end in 15 minutes," you must look at how the character reacts to that statement. Your opinion does not matter. You may look at that and see one conflict, but another person may see a different conflict.

That's why conflict is not left up to the viewer. It relies solely on the response of the main character. If the character responds, "I don't care," then there's no conflict within the storyline of the world ending. The character needs to care. How much the character cares will determine what the conflict is. If the main character cares more about getting a girl to like him as opposed to the world ending, your major conflict lies with the girl, not the world. As hard as it may be to detach yourself from your personal opinion, it's the nature of conflict that it belongs to the character. Leaving conflict up to the main character's perception helps determine which conflict is more apparent and present in the story.

Multiple conflicts can happen simultaneously. All six types, in fact, can be present in the right story. This is an important concept to understand: When conflicts start to intersect, that's when you really rely on the main character for guidance. The character may care more about one conflict or the other. This is how shot selection and conflict are directly related.

▶ MULTIPLE CONFLICTS AT WORK

The film *The Aviator,* a story about Howard Hughes, has a few conflicts. Hughes's business manager is constantly telling him he's going to lose all his money. That may seem like an important conflict, but Hughes is more concerned with pushing the limits with his particular projects. These projects mostly have to do with movies and airplanes. At one point, when they finally finish shooting the movie *Hell's Angels,* Hughes tells his manager he wants to reshoot the movie for sound. It's very clear in this moment that Hughes cares only about finishing the movie and proving people wrong—not about losing his money.

Those are the rules of conflict. To sum up:

- No conflict, no plot.
- It's all about the main character's perception of conflict. That individual must care about the problem to have conflict.
- Multiple conflicts can be happening simultaneously.

Before we get into the link between conflict and shot selection, let's first understand the six types of conflicts.

▶ **ACCESSING THE DOWNLOADS FOR THIS BOOK**

While describing these six types of conflicts, I refer to specific timecodes from this book's companion film *Out Of Order*. These timecodes tell you where you can find a scene that deals with each specific conflict. Remember, a film has an overall conflict, but each scene has its own arc and its own conflict as well. See this book's Introduction for more about the companion movie and how to access the free download.

Relational Conflict (Human vs. Human)

Relational conflict, also known as human versus human, is the most common of the six conflicts (**FIGURE 2.1**). This conflict simply consists of two characters in the story who are trying to achieve the same—or opposite—goals. One is the *protagonist,* often the hero of the story. This is the character the audience is supposed to root for, empathize with, and relate to. However, that doesn't have to be the case. (Shot selection feeds this theory, as explored later in the chapter.)

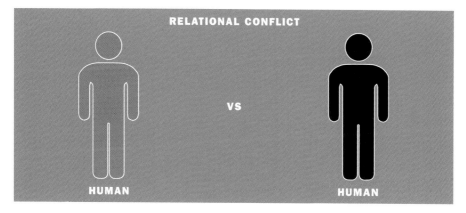

FIGURE 2.1 Relational conflict, sometimes referred to as human versus human conflict, is the most common of the six conflicts.

The other participant in the conflict is the *antagonist,* often called the villain. The audience is supposed to root against this character, but that's not always the case either.

Relational conflict can take many forms of human versus human. Some examples include:

- Two characters in the story who are trying to achieve the same goal.

- The protagonist wants to accomplish a goal; the antagonist wants to prevent the protagonist from accomplishing that goal.

- The protagonist plays for a team. In that case, the antagonist might be the entire opposing team, but it is often represented by one central character. It's important to note that the antagonist is not always just one character; it can be many characters, a group, or an institution. Think about a story such as *Game of Thrones*. This is a story that includes many substories. Think about the characters at The Wall. Their antagonists are the White Walkers, which are represented by no single character.

At times, conflict becomes confusing in the sense that the word "conflict" is immediately associated with events that are negative. Negativity, however, is not necessarily the case. Two characters in a story playing a simple board game can represent relational conflict. Both characters are trying to achieve the same goal of winning the game. In situations such as that, you could almost flip a coin regarding which is the protagonist and which is the antagonist. In that case, the only thing leading the viewers to empathize with one character or the other is the shot selection. This is one of the many reasons shot selection and conflict is related.

OUT OF ORDER MOVIE *The timecode 00:00 is the beginning of the film and the best example of relational conflict. The simple fact that two characters sit across from each other is symbolic. This interview scene, which runs throughout the movie, is a great example of relational conflict. The female interviewer, Alex, is trying to rattle Paul in the interview to make for a better story in her film, and Paul is trying to stay calm, cool, and collected so he looks good in the film and doesn't show his true colors (**FIGURE 2.2**).*

FIGURE 2.2 Paul is the protagonist and Alex is the antagonist in *Out of Order.*

Here are three examples of movies with relational conflict:

The Social Network: In this film, the main character is being sued by his best friend for stealing the idea for Facebook. He's also being sued by a group of three people who claim he stole their idea for Facebook. The conflict is still relational, and it's between the main character and his best friend because this is what the main character cares about.

The Dark Night: This movie is about a lot of things, but nothing more so than the Joker versus Batman. In this case, Batman is trying to save Gotham City, and the Joker is trying to prevent him from accomplishing that goal.

The Prestige: This is a movie about two magicians on a quest to be the best. The competition here is who can be the best while sacrificing the least.

Social Conflict (Human vs. Group)

Social conflict, also known as human versus group, is very common and pretty self-explanatory (**FIGURE 2.3**). The conflict consists primarily of one human opposing an entire group of people, which collectively plays the role of the antagonist. The opposing group does not need to be developed, only represented, which can even be known as human versus idea. An example of social conflict is *The Hunger Games*. In this film, Katniss is opposing the government. Sure, she's in the competition against her opponents, which would still fall under social conflict, but she's actually opposing the entire idea of *The Hunger Games*.

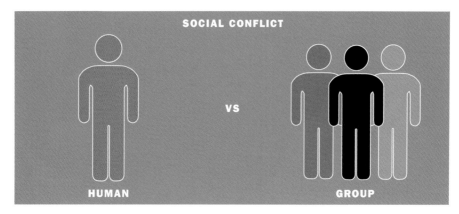

FIGURE 2.3 Social conflict, also known as human versus group, is a common conflict in stories.

There is a bit of overlap here. I *did* mention human versus an entire opposing team in the discussion of relational conflict. The reason some of those still fall under relational conflict is because, usually, a team is part of a league. In that example the league would be the group, and the team would be treated as a developed character. Also, a central character represents the team. The human versus idea example that falls into human versus group is different in the sense that there is no representative for the group.

Think of any war movie. The opposing country would be the antagonist. There doesn't need to be an extension of that country that is personally developed (although, of course, there can be and often is). The overlap line here is admittedly pretty thin. When trying to understand the difference, you should rely on one of the rules of conflict: Look at the conflict through the main character's point of view. Is he singling out an idea or a specific person who is part of the idea? This is the deciding factor.

Here are some examples with social conflict:

- A protagonist needs the cooperation of a group he's not fond of to complete his personal goal.

- The group does not like the protagonist, making it harder to accomplish his goal.

- To accomplish his goal, the protagonist must unite a group of people who may or may not be fond of each other.

Remember, conflict is not always negative. A character could be trying to convince a group of people to work together and that's it. They may not have a problem with each other.

OUT OF ORDER MOVIE *The scene at timecode 34:51 is a perfect example of social conflict. It doesn't fall into any of the three examples mentioned in this section, but it is still social conflict. Paul is trying to convince a group of people that his idea is good in hopes they'll change the entire direction of their company. The group isn't opposed to the idea, in the traditional sense of the word, so the element of convincing still exists. Otherwise, the scene wouldn't need to exist in the first place (**FIGURE 2.4**).*

FIGURE 2.4 An example of social conflict is seen in *Out of Order* when Paul tries to convince the company about his idea.

Here are three examples of movies with social conflict:

Dallas Buyers Club: This is a story about a man infected with HIV who starts selling memberships to a club that provides people with drugs to manage HIV symptoms. The U.S. government tries repeatedly to shut him down.

Any Given Sunday: This is about a football coach who tries to unite his team and drown out any distractions in hopes of keeping his job and making the playoffs.

Remember the Titans: In this football movie, the group is much bigger than the team because the elements of segregation are at play. This is more than just a coach uniting the team. This is the team—with the coach as its representative—uniting a whole town.

Situational Conflict (Human vs. Environment)

Situational conflict, also known as human versus environment, can get a little confusing (**FIGURE 2.5**). Humans face a conflict with the environment, which often causes characters to disagree about how to handle that conflict. Situational conflict often gets overlooked (and grouped with relational conflict) because the characters disagree. There is an easy way to determine whether a conflict is relational or situational: If your characters are having a disagreement about the environment or the conditions they've been presented by the environment, then the conflict is situational.

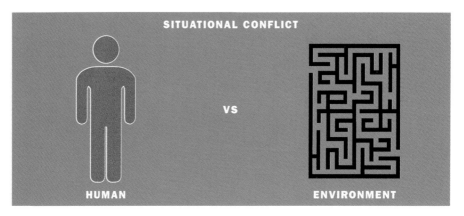

FIGURE 2.5 Situational conflict, also known as human versus environment, can get confused with relational conflict.

Here's the rule: The environment introduces the conflict, and then the characters have disagreements among themselves about the conditions the environment has presented. When characters in the story disagree, that's conflict. You need to dig into the source of the disagreement. If the environment has presented the initial conditions, it's a situational conflict.

Let's look at an example of how relational conflict can be confused with situational conflict. Characters are trapped inside a burning building and they disagree on their plan of exit. As an editor, you *must* be able to tell the difference between conflicts because the conflict ties directly into shot selection.

Here are some other examples of situational conflict:

- A group of characters is lost in the woods, and the group is split on how to find the way out.

- Two characters are in a bad car accident. One thinks they should climb out of the crashed car, and the other thinks they should stay and wait for help to arrive.

- It rains the morning of an outdoor wedding, and the bride and groom must overcome the conditions to continue with the event.

These examples are all very different, but they all fall into the category of situational conflict. The first example, a group lost in the woods, is the one that introduces overlap. Being lost in the woods isn't necessarily a life or death situation, so the drama is among the characters. (Often, situational conflict *is* a life or death situation, but it's doesn't have to be.) The second example, of the car accident, does fall into a more serious scenario. This conflict has the overlapping conflict of two characters with different theories on how to handle the conflict the environment has presented. The real drama, however, lies with the actual car crash. The third example, the rainy wedding, deals with uniting the characters in an effort to handle the conflict of the environment. All three are unique and fall into human versus environment conflict.

When trying to apply situational conflict to a real-world situation, such as a wedding or an event, remember this: Look through the eyes of your main characters. First, you will need to identify the main characters. Then, find the conflict that they see. In a wedding film, finding this type of conflict is rare, because if something is going wrong with the environment, chances are you don't want to highlight it. For example, if you are filming an outdoor wedding and it starts raining, you don't want to make the film about that!

However, in some situations, highlighting the environment is plausible. When I made my first wedding video, a long time ago in Italy, I did this. The couple was getting married in a pedestrian-only part of town—no cars allowed. I chose to take their journey to the town, make a story out of it, and relate it to their love. I used the visual adventure as conflict and linked the couple together in overcoming the conflict. Remember, it's not always about what you shoot—it's how it's presented in the edit.

Here are a few examples of movies with situational conflict:

Titanic: This is a love story first and foremost, but the drama is in the sinking ship. This falls in line with the wedding example cited previously. The two characters are falling in love, and the sinking ship unites them even more.

This Is the End: This is an interesting case study on determining the most prominent conflict in a story. The movie is about a group of characters trapped inside a house during the apocalypse. At first glance, it could be categorized as cosmic conflict (human versus destiny, discussed later in the chapter). If you look closer, however, the more prominent conflict is situational. Why? When looking through the eyes of the characters, they aren't entirely sure of what's happening. It takes until the end of the film to even determine what happened. This is not really a movie about trying to survive as much as it is a movie about the characters' disagreements spawning from the environment they are trapped in. Again, multiple conflicts can be happening at the same time, but as the editor, you need to know which one trumps all in order to determine your shot selection.

Argo: This is a clear-cut case of situational conflict. A group of Americans are trapped abroad, and who better to break them out than a CIA agent played by Ben Affleck? This movie causes an array of drama between the group that's trapped for fear of being discovered and killed trying to escape.

Inner Conflict (Human vs. Self)

Inner conflict, also known as human versus self, is very common as well (**FIGURE 2.6**). Usually, inner conflict is not a main conflict, but it acts as a way to develop a strong main character. With inner conflict, the main character is in a struggle with herself. This is a modern-day storytelling technique, and it usually consists of a flawed main character. A flawed character doesn't have to be associated with something evil or negative—it could be a passive character or someone who lacks confidence.

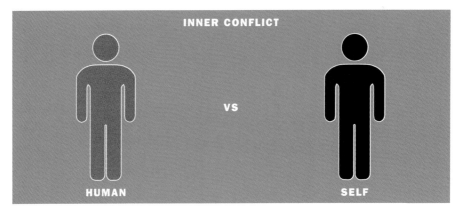

FIGURE 2.6 Inner conflict, also known as human versus self, is usually present on some level in every story.

Here are some examples of inner conflict:

- A protagonist is in love with someone, but she lacks the confidence to approach him and confess her feelings.

- A protagonist wants to write his bride a letter on their wedding day, but he can't think of the right words to say and struggles to write the letter.

- A protagonist struggles with guilt about something he did in the past, and it affects his present affairs.

- A protagonist has obsessive-compulsive disorder (OCD) and can't get it under control, thus affecting her current life decisions.

While inner conflict may be present, it's not often the main conflict. Remember, it's all about the main character's perception of the conflict. Let's say the main character is at a bar and sees a woman he thinks is attractive. If it takes him only a few minutes to overcome being shy before he talks to her, then inner conflict is not the main conflict in the story. However, overcoming shyness may be the conflict for that particular scene. Remember, every scene has an arc and every arc has a conflict. Sometimes, a scene has its own conflict, which always feeds the bigger story arc's conflict.

To clarify: Every story has a conflict, sometimes multiple conflicts, and the editor must treat each scene as a separate story arc when it comes to shot selection. Using the example of the man approaching the women at the bar, that scene's conflict might be inner conflict, but the overall story may have nothing to do with the inner conflict in this particular scene. This is why understanding the story arc is important. As the editor, you need to know where to divert the audience's attention and show them what to focus on. You do this through shot selection, covered later in this chapter.

> *Conflict doesn't always have to be negative or even extreme. It can be simple.*

Like any conflict, inner conflict can relate to any type of film. For a wedding, inner conflict can be everywhere. Maybe your groom is trying to write a letter to his bride and can't think of the words to say. That's inner conflict. Remember, inner conflict doesn't always have to be negative or even extreme. It can be simple.

OUT OF ORDER MOVIE Toward the end of Out of Order, *at timecode 01:27, is a scene when Brice is fired. It's interesting because this scene is a relational conflict, from the beginning of the scene to about this point in the scene. Once Brice is fired, the conflict has been resolved, and we move on to a new conflict. Inner conflict becomes the main attraction here because Paul is clearly disturbed by his decision to fire his best friend Brice. This is the nature of conflicts that move from scene to scene as opposed to the conflict throughout a whole film. Each scene must bleed into the next scene and flow. It's natural to introduce to conflict at the end of a scene that will be the focal point of the next scene (**FIGURE 2.7**).*

FIGURE 2.7 You can see inner conflict in *Out of Order* when Paul feels bad about firing Brice.

Here are some examples of movies with inner conflict:

The Aviator: This film's execution of tying shot selection to conflict is unlike any film I have ever seen. You could make an argument that every conflict on the list is present in this story. And you'd be right. But Howard Hughes's OCD trumps them all. If you watch this film with OCD in mind, notice the shot selection choices the editor makes when Hughes has an OCD outburst: close-up shots. Close-ups make these moments more intense, which reinforces the story's conflict to the viewer. (More on this later in this chapter.)

The Matrix: You might think this movie is more of a case of situational conflict. Although that's not wrong, human versus environment is not more apparent than Neo's inner struggle, which is inner conflict. Inner conflict trumps all conflicts in this story because this story is really about a computer hacker who must come to terms with the fact that he's *the one*. Only then can the story transition into the resolution part of the story arc.

Fight Club: This is my all-time favorite movie. It has more layers than any film I've ever seen. It, too, is about inner conflict. In fact, *Fight Club* might be the case study for films with inner conflict. The main character is in a struggle with himself, literally. The unnamed main character is pretending to be his counterpart, Tyler Durden. When you find out Tyler is all in the main character's head, it's a great example of a *reveal* (a plot twist, discussed in Chapter 1).

Cosmic Conflict (Human vs. Destiny or Fate)

Cosmic conflict, also known as human versus destiny or fate, is easily the trickiest one of the six conflicts (**FIGURE 2.8**). All it takes to establish cosmic conflict is for the main character to say one line that introduces the idea of battling fate. The key is to look for the character to say anything having to do with fate. All it takes is a line such as:

- "No more existence."
- "Are we safe?"
- "I don't want to die."
- "I want to be with you forever."

This has limits like anything else. The line must be spoken when characters are discussing the central point of the story.

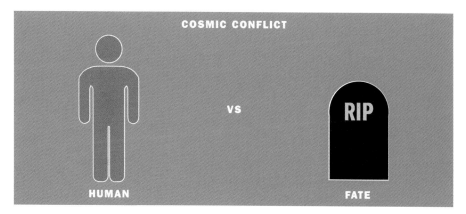

FIGURE 2.8 Cosmic conflict, also known as human versus destiny, is the trickiest of the six. Rely on your main character's perception of conflict to determine what the conflict really is. In this case, watch for the main character to say something about fate.

These lines deal with the abstract idea of future situations. Often, cosmic conflict can be confused with situational conflict. If the character is trying to prevent or create something in the future, the story must deal with fate. Another key to remember is that this conflict does not have to be resolved. Unresolved conflict is still conflict.

Here are some examples:

- A protagonist begs God's forgiveness to get into heaven when he dies. He does not need to be forgiven when he asks; all he needs to do is believe there is a God and beg.

- A protagonist is fighting terminal cancer and tries to prevent her inevitable death with experimental treatment.

- A main character thinks that by deleting his Facebook account, people will forget who he is.

- A main character buys a safe car in case of a car crash. This way, she is prepared for the future.

- A main character is determined to finish college because he believes it will land him a good job when he graduates.

Like the situational conflict, cosmic conflict is usually dramatic or life threatening, but it doesn't have to be. This all rests on the main character's perception of the conflict. If the main character tries—in any way—to alter the past or future (or even want to), then you have cosmic conflict.

> **OUT OF ORDER MOVIE** *The scene at timecode 1:20:54 is a great example of cosmic conflict. In this scene, Paul and John are trying to change the future by advancing technology. It's important to watch this scene in full because a natural assumption is that it's going to be human versus technology (described in the next section), but it's not. This scene features cosmic conflict because it's told through the eyes of Paul, who thinks what they are trying to do is possible (**FIGURE 2.9**).*

FIGURE 2.9 In *Out of Order,* when Paul discusses changes in videography and video editing—and believes in it—with his boss, it's a great example of cosmic conflict.

Here are some examples of movies with cosmic conflict:

Déjà Vu: The main character must use time travel to alter the past in order to change the future. No one believes a human can be sent back in time, but the characters still take a leap of faith and try to see if they can alter the future.

Gravity: This film seems like it would involve situational conflict—and the situational element is clearly present. However, the fact is that the main character is trapped in space, and if she doesn't do something about it, she's going to die. Her decisions in the film are based on avoiding her inevitable death.

25th Hour: This movie is about a man trying to get his affairs in order before he goes to prison for eight years. It is an interesting way to use cosmic conflict because his fate is already decided. His one option to change it is to run. The film is a constant study and contemplation of that option.

Paranormal Conflict (Human vs. Technology)

Paranormal conflict, also known as human versus technology, is the most misleading conflict of them all (**FIGURE 2.10**). Don't be confused by the words *paranormal* or *technology*—it's unfortunate that this is the terminology, but it is. Paranormal conflict actually has nothing to do with ghosts or iPads. The primary definition of this conflict is that the main character is pushing the limits of what she believes to be *possible*. This is so important to understand because the moment people see computers or gadgets in a story, they default to believing the conflict is paranormal. That's a common mistake and can result in mixed signals when it comes to shot selection.

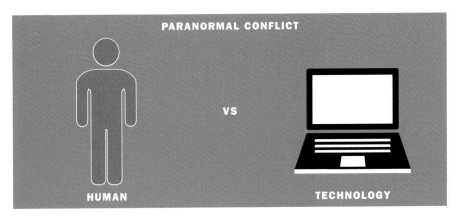

FIGURE 2.10 Paranormal conflict is about the main character pushing the limits of what he believes to be possible.

How can you tell if it's paranormal conflict? The key is the main character's perception. If the main character in the story believes what he is trying to accomplish is possible, then it's not paranormal conflict. If the main character believes he can fly, then the conflict is human versus environment. If he isn't convinced it's possible to fly, then it's paranormal conflict.

Here's the important difference: We, the audience, know that sending a toy airplane into space is scientifically impossible. But the world of a story isn't always our world, so it doesn't matter what we think or know. If the main character believes he *can* do it, it's no longer a paranormal conflict. If the main character wants to *try* to fly a toy plane into space and isn't sure whether it will work, you have paranormal conflict.

What's the difference? Paranormal conflict has the main character pushing the limits of what he believes to be possible.

Here are some examples:

- A protagonist wants to break the world record in the 100-meter dash, but he isn't sure he can do it.
- A protagonist wants to build a time machine, but she isn't sure if it will work.
- A protagonist wants to build a self-driving car, but he isn't convinced it's possible.

Again, it's all about the main character's perception of conflict. If she doubts the possibility, it's paranormal conflict.

> **OUT OF ORDER MOVIE** *No need for a timecode here because* Out of Order, *in its entirety, is about human versus technology! Paul pushes the limits of what he believes to be possible from the very beginning.*

Here are some examples of movies with paranormal conflict:

Moneyball: This is a great example of paranormal conflict. Brad Pitt's character is trying an unconventional way of assembling a baseball team that nobody, including him, is convinced is possible.

Out of Order: This is about the man who invented the first digital video editing system. No one thought it was possible, and behind closed doors, even the main character had doubts about whether it would work.

Inception: In this film, the characters are trying to hack into people's minds and plant thoughts inside. The main character must convince himself and his team that "inception" is possible.

Why does all this matter? Because of shot selection. You must be able to determine the conflict while you are editing. Shot selection is a key element of editing, and it has the biggest psychological effect on the viewing experience. Nothing in shot selection should be random. Every shot should have a purpose and a reason. It's important to be in complete control of the viewers and steer their attention and emotions in the right place at the right time.

Shot Selection

If a ranking system existed for the most important editing tasks, shot selection would come in a close second place to pacing (the timing of cuts, explored in Chapter 4). If a ranking system existed for the most overlooked and misunderstood editing tasks, shot selection would be a runaway for number one.

When everything is filmed and it's time to piece everything together on the timeline, many editors use a random calculation for the shots they choose to include in the film. Sometimes, the decisions are made by feel or instinct, and many times a naturally gifted editor's instincts are correct. Instinct won't work every single time, though, especially when you're a beginner. You can't rely on instinct for consistency in shot selection.

Having said that, it isn't an exact science, and instinct does play a role in the art of shot selection. But what you must understand is the psychological outcomes of the decisions you're making. If you're going to choose a shot to cut to, you need to know the meaning of the shot, and you need to know what will happen to the viewer's mind when the sequence of shots comes together.

Many editors—especially beginners who don't have the right instincts yet—follow a predictable pattern. They may edit a conversation scene the same way every time, for example, no matter where they are in the plot arc or what the conflict is. When you ask yourself, "What shot should I choose here?" you should also be asking, "What is the conflict?" This doesn't mean conflict is the single determining factor in shot selection, but it should be heavily considered.

That goes for any film. I'm currently editing an event film consisting of speeches to end world hunger. I recorded eight hours of speeches to make a five-minute film. And I'm using the same philosophy when it comes to shot selection that I would in a feature film: "Where am I in the plot arc, and what's the conflict?" If I determine I'm at the climax, and the conflict is being directly referenced in a particular part of a speech, then my shot selection is different than if it was not referenced. Later in the chapter I explain how my shot selection is affected by what's being said in the narrative and whether it feeds the conflict of the story.

A great editor is one who mixes instinct with *pattern* while sprinkling in a little science. (*Pattern* is editing similar scenes with the same type of shots across the story.) Pattern can be a part of shot selection, but it's not the whole pie. You can use pattern to edit scenes across the story that are similar in nature and mirror that with repetitive shot selection, but that's where pattern runs its course in terms of using it for shot selection. Here's how you can effectively combine pattern, instinct, and science:

- Pattern. Using pattern to draw a viewer's attention to a particular plot point is effective. Seeing the same type of shots linked with the same type of emotions, conflict, and plot points gives viewers a visual reference of what a particular conflict looks like.

- Instinct. The use of instinct is simply put: "Does this feel right?" Another word for instinct is *style*. Over time, you'll develop a style for shot selection.

- Science. Science refers to the meaning and uses for the four different types of shots: wide, medium, close-up, and B-roll. Each type of shot has a particular use. For example, a wide shot is used to establish the setting. That doesn't mean you always need to establish the setting with a wide shot. When I say science, I want you to think of the *recommended use* for a particular shot— but always remember this is art.

▶ KNOW THE RULE BEFORE YOU BREAK IT

The science of shot selection involves *choosing the scientifically correct shot to match the conflict*. (This topic is covered later in this chapter.) Choosing to ignore the science is an artistic choice you'll make often, but you should have a rational reason for ignoring the science. It's the old "You have to know the rule before you can break it" idea. Otherwise, you're playing a guessing game. And guessing wrong either steers your viewers in the wrong direction or doesn't feed the major goal that is your story's desired emotion.

Keep in mind that shot selection is not about the *timing* of the cuts—that's pacing. Shot selection is knowing the proper shot to cut to when you are deciding to make a cut. First, you must know the purpose of each shot. Then, you apply that to the conflict. For the purposes of learning the importance of shot selection, I'll assume you have the clips you need to make the proper decisions during editing.

Wide Shots

The wide shot, shown in **FIGURE 2.11**, is mostly used for establishing everything in a scene, including:

- Characters
- Characters' positions in relation to one another
- Lighting
- Layout of the room or environment
- Context

FIGURE 2.11 The wide shot shows the overall setting and all the characters present. You use this shot to establish.

Because most stories are told through the eyes of the characters, character is a logical place to start when thinking about establishing. This goes for the main characters—all the way down to the most meaningless extra you may have in your story.

ESTABLISHING WHO AND WHAT IS IN THE SCENE

It's important to give the viewers an overview of *who* or *what* is in the room where the scene is taking place, regardless of whether who or what is in the room is an important part of the moment. For example, if a wide shot has six characters sitting around a table but the scene is about only two of those six characters, then the wide shot becomes important because it gives the viewers information about who's important and who's not (once it's mixed in with other types of shots, which are likely close-ups of the two important people). If you start a scene with a wide shot showing six people but the viewers never (or rarely) sees four of those people again, the viewers know not to identify with those four people. As viewers, we know to ignore them. We never have the opportunity to empathize with them.

Maybe we keep seeing a third character's reaction throughout the scene. We know that in some way, shape, or form, that character must be important. (By the way, this is why the concept of *B-roll* is so misunderstood. There's no such thing as a shot that doesn't mean something. More on B-roll later in this chapter.)

Establishing the characters' positions in relation to one another can't be overlooked. The more details the viewers know about the characters' positions, the less you need to establish later on. (By positions, I mean such things as character A is sitting across from character B, and the door to the room is behind character B.)

As far as shots go, the wide shot contains the least amount of emotion but the most amount of information about the overall scene layout. Remember: There is no emotion in a wide shot, only information. If you do a good job of telling the audience where characters are in the scene, you'll need fewer shots to establish that later on in the scene. The viewers need to have a subconscious understanding of how the scene is laid out.

Remember that you are trying to re-create reality. The fewer questions the audience has about that reality, the better the film. Let them focus on what matters—the story and the characters. The more you can avoid needing to establish the characters' positions in the middle of a scene, the better off you'll be. Therefore, wide shots are usually used at the beginning of a scene. If you build up emotion in a scene, using a wide shot later can quickly damage the emotion you've created. This is because there is nowhere to focus your attention, emotion, or empathy—in contrast to the close-up or medium shot.

Use the wide shot briefly and when the timing is right. Holding on a wide shot drains the emotion from the scene. The viewers start to look at the overall scene as opposed to empathizing with the characters. Of course, there are times when you want the audience to do just that, as you'll find out later in this section. If you're trying to create a really long shot or a take, known as a *one take*, that's a different scenario (explored later in the chapter).

ESTABLISHING LIGHTING

Lighting is another thing to establish with a wide shot. This is one of those points that can vary from filmmaker to filmmaker, and I'll admit it's a personal preference of mine. Justify your lighting. Show where the light sources are coming from in the room. Nothing takes viewers out of the story quicker than a light that makes absolutely no sense inside the scene they're watching. Providing a quick context of light placement and showing the *practical* lights goes a long way toward explaining why the light looks a certain way.

> **NOTE** In film, practical lights are the lamps or natural light coming in through windows in the room. They give the room a sense of realism. The filmmaker's light should join in with the practical lights.

If the viewers know where and what each light source is in a room, there is no need to further justify the light. However, when the lighting is out of the norm, you need to justify it. A good example of this concept is a bedroom scene at night. If there are no lamps on in the room, then what is the light source? This is usually when you see a bright white light shining through the window, conveniently situated next to the bed. Of course, we all know that not every bed is placed perfectly next to a window, and not every window allows a bright streetlight to shine into the bedroom. Movies would have us think otherwise. Think about the concept. In reality, that light would be the worst thing ever because how could you every get any sleep with that bright light shining in the room? It's borderline unrealistic to have that light source, yet it's one of the only options. If you do set up lights that mimic the look of a streetlight, then show the viewers the window in a wide shot so they know what that light is and where it's coming from. Doing that will go a long way toward making the scene feel real. Granted, this all applies if you choose to care about justifying your lighting in the first place.

Take a look at **FIGURES 2.12** and **2.13**. In Figure 2.12, the lighting pattern cast on the wall behind the character makes no sense at all. Nowhere on planet Earth is that a natural lighting pattern. But if you look at Figure 2.13, which is the reverse angle of this shot, you see that the light coming from that direction is the lamp in the far back of the room, and the pattern is created by the stairs blocking the light. While this isn't literally true, it's how you get the viewers to believe the artificial lighting.

FIGURE 2.12 A lighting pattern on the wall adds depth to the scene, but it needs justification in the editing. You justify it by showing the source of light in the reverse angle.

FIGURE 2.13 The reverse angle and the light source from the lamp are broken by the steps. As long as you edit them together, viewers will make sense of it in their minds.

ESTABLISHING THE LAYOUT OF THE SCENE

The layout of the room is an important concept for all scenes, whether or not it plays a role in the scene. This is something to focus on as an editor. The dialogue of a scene often begins while the viewers are still looking at shots of the room the characters are entering. The purpose for this is to mimic what happens when anybody walks into a place for the first time—they look around and get their bearings. They look up, they look down, they look at the decor, photographs, signs, and television. Essentially, they look at any details that make the room unique. In real life, we do this even more than a film would choose to show us, but the idea is to mimic at least a little of what we do in real life. Give the viewers that sense of realism. The more details you give them, the more you mimic their actions of observation, and the more they will buy into the false reality you're trying to sell them.

As mentioned in Chapter 1, movies often start with a sequence of establishing shots of a city. The sequence paints a broad picture for the viewers about where they are, and the viewers fill in the rest. You can choose to not provide the viewers such a layout as well. However, choosing to go this route should be for a specific desired outcome. Maybe you don't want the viewers to know anything about the surrounding environment, which might make them a little uneasy. If the goal of a scene is to make the viewers feel uneasy or disoriented, then not showing the setting in a wide shot may be a good choice. Maybe the layout doesn't matter and plays no part in the scene whatsoever. Then it's a coin flip and comes down to style. If the location plays a part in the story, showing the layout is an important goal to accomplish.

ESTABLISHING CONTEXT

At the beginning of every scene you need context. Context falls under every point made about wide shots. Show me where the characters are, how the room is lit (which will establish mood), where the characters are sitting or standing, and the layout of the room. All that falls into context. The thing with context is that it always changes if your story is following an arc. When the context changes, it's important to treat it as if the scene has restarted, visually, and the viewers need to be reintroduced to certain elements of the scene.

For example, let's say you have two characters in a room talking about the weather. First, you use a wide shot to establish and then edit the scene. Normally, you wouldn't use a wide shot in the middle of a conversation scene because the wide shot carries no intensity. This philosophy has two exceptions.

- To remove the intensity, you could opt for a wide shot of a conversation scene.
- To indicate a change in topic, you might show a wide shot. For example, suppose the conversation switches from talking about the weather to talking about plans to rob a bank. When the new topic starts, I'd treat that as a new scene and start with a wide shot. Or, depending on how long they talk about the weather, I'd hold on a wide shot while they are talking about the weather, and move to more intense shots when the topic changes. Either option works and accomplishes the visual change the viewers need to be drawn into the scene.

Context can change, and it may need to be re-established at any point during a scene. Context can be as simple as a character's movement. A character can be sitting, and when he goes to stand up, you may want to show a wide shot and establish his new position. In any event, context is the primary reason for using wide shots. Context is the major component of establishing. Don't let the viewers forget the context of the moment they are in—or they may forget why they are there in the first place.

Medium Shots

The medium shot is just as its name suggests: It's the happy medium between a wide shot and a close-up shot. It's wide enough to give a bit of context while close enough to draw your attention to a specific subject (see **FIGURE 2.14**). The medium shot singles out what is to be the focus of the scene. For instance, say you have those same six characters as mentioned in the wide shot example. Of those six, two are important. Following the wide shot, you would show one or more medium shots of the two characters the scene will focus on.

A medium shot draws attention to a particular subject (or two). It allows the viewers to ignore the overwhelming amount of information in a wide shot and focus on the details in the subject. However, a medium shot is not so close that the viewers forget things such as context. We can still see some of the background activity that happens in the room while focusing on a particular subject.

The medium shot will be your most commonly used type of shot. This is because context and emotion don't need to be constantly established.

FIGURE 2.14 The medium shot shows more of a subject than a close-up and is your most-used shot. Compared to a wide shot, a medium shot singles out what is important.

SHOWING EMOTION

Close-up shots are where intense emotions come from, but the medium shot can still be used to convey emotion. The framing put us close enough to the subject's face to see emotion and expression, but far enough away that it gives us context of body movement. And body movement plays a huge role in conveying the emotion of a scene. When it comes to a subject that is not a person, the same rules apply. Medium shots help single out the details of the subject.

GIVING A SENSE OF CONTEXT

You still get a small sense of the context from a medium shot. If the wide shot shows five characters chopping wood with axes outside on a hot summer day, then the medium shot would single out one of those characters while still showing a few of the five characters in the background. In those moments, the brain will recall the image of the wide shot to retain context. The medium shot means you don't need to remind the viewers about who is there and where they are. You can focus on giving viewers new details about the moment and really concentrate on forcing their attention to a particular character.

The same brain function applies if you re-create the wood-chopping scene in reverse. Let's say you show the medium shot of the man chopping wood with a few other guys in the background doing the same thing. Then you show the context (wide shot) after a character has already been established. Same idea, different emotion. We already made a connection to the man chopping wood because it was the first image we saw. Using a wide then medium shot gives us a moment, and then tells us who's important. We don't know what's important while watching the wide shot. We simply take in the moment as a whole. Then the medium shot shows us who is important and the brain switches its focus to that particular character.

Using the medium-then-wide shot order is an entirely different method. We first learn whom the scene is about and then we see the context and view that wide shot with a different purpose. Now we want to see how our subject fits into the context that is being established. The simple order of two shots changes the viewing experience. There is no right or wrong way, but each choice you make should contribute to a goal, and each choice carries implications for the viewer. I explore that goal in Chapter 3. For now, just note the power of the medium shot. It can change the way you view a wide shot simply by where in the sequence you place it.

Close-ups

The close-up is the window to the soul. If you're trying to deliver a character's emotion to a viewer, a close-up is the most powerful shot you can show. Close-ups are how you make your emotional point and punctuate the scene.

The close-up works exactly like a drug. The more you use it, the less it's going to work. This is why it's important to have a balance when it comes to shot selection. If you have a film that's heavy on close-ups, you have no contrast for the viewers to determine what's important and what's not.

At times, editors struggle to resist the use of a close-up in a particular moment because close-ups tend to be created with the most cinematic of lenses. Just because something looks good, that doesn't mean you should use it.

TYPES AND TIMING OF CLOSE-UPS

There are two types of close-ups: the close-up (CU) shown in **FIGURE 2.15** and the extreme close-up (ECU) shown in **FIGURE 2.16**. The close-up is the more common of the two. Think of it this way: The further you move into a subject, the more you focus on the subject's expression, and the less context you have about the particular setting. Extreme close-ups are almost always used in surreal settings to make you forget where you are and focus on only one particular thing, whereas close-ups offer a more realistic viewpoint of a character's emotions. This comes down to a stylistic choice more than anything, but there is a time and a place for the use of extreme close-ups as discussed later in this chapter.

FIGURE 2.15 A close-up shot is used in a similar manner to an extreme close-up, except it's a little wider and doesn't draw you to the eyes nearly as much. It's more about looking at the face or important features of a subject.

FIGURE 2.16 The extreme close-up offers an almost *surreal* view of a subject. In this image, it draws the viewers to connect with the subject on a deep level through the eyes. This view or anything closer is considered an extreme close-up.

There are a few ways to time close-ups, and they also fall into the realm of stylistic choices. You can use close-ups on the most emotional lines or moments of the scene, or directly *after* the most emotional lines of the scene or moment. Either way, the close-up is used in relation to the most emotional line or moment.

> **TIP** *In my opinion, a significant consideration regarding whether to use a close-up during or directly after an emotional moment is the caliber of the actors. If the actor is good enough to convincingly pull off the emotion during the scene, show the close-up during.*

You can use close-ups for a wide range of purposes:

- Reinforcing the protagonist in a third-person narrative
- Isolating emotions from a big group
- Isolating important elements
- Reinforcing the conflict

These uses—which are often forgotten when it comes to shot selection—are explained in the following sections.

REINFORCING THE PROTAGONIST IN A THIRD-PERSON NARRATIVE

Reinforcing who the protagonist is during a third-person narrative is imperative. Chapter 3 covers narrative perspective, but understanding that the editor has this power is important. When the viewers don't know who to identify with, you can lead them in the right direction with a series of contrasting shots. Close-ups help you identify with a character's emotion in a slightly different way than medium shots. If a scene cuts back and forth between two characters using several close-ups of one character and several medium shots of the other character, it almost forces the viewers to identify with the character shown in the close-ups. The viewers don't empathize as much with the character in the medium shots.

If you look at the two shots in **FIGURES 2.17** and **2.18**, you'll see it's easy to determine the emotion in the close-up shot, whereas the medium shot has more context. This is not to say a medium shot can't convey emotion—because it certainly can—but when it's next to a close-up, there's no contest. The viewers are drawn to empathize with the subject of the close-up shot.

FIGURE 2.17 In this close-up, the only thing viewers can focus on is his expression. It's intense partly because of the expression and partly because there is nothing else to take away from this image.

FIGURE 2.18 This medium shot doesn't produce nearly the same effect as a close-up would. We still can take away some emotion, but we have a bit more context about the setting and the character's body language. His face is not the only focal point. The viewers have a little more freedom to interpret emotion.

ISOLATING EMOTIONS FROM A BIG GROUP

Isolating emotions from a big group is the same philosophy as isolating who is important from a big group, only with different shots. You can single out who is important by showing a medium shot of a character after they've been seen in a wide shot. The same thing can happen with isolating emotion.

Show a wide shot (**FIGURE 2.19**), then follow with a close-up shot (**FIGURE 2.20**), and the viewers immediately isolate the different emotions in the room and focus their energy on the shot you show.

The major difference between using a close-up and an extreme close-up is *when* you do this. You'll often be singling out *who* is important early on in the scene, and later in the scene you'll be singling out the *emotion* that is important. Often, this occurs in the middle of the scene when you re-establish context for the viewer. You show a wide shot that gives the viewers context, but contains the least amount of emotion, then you hit them with the close-up that isolates the emotion of the wide shot and brings the viewers right back into the emotion of the scene.

ISOLATING IMPORTANT ELEMENTS

Isolating objects is a simple concept. If there is something in a scene that is important, chances are you'll want to give the viewers a close-up view of the object. Doing so focuses their attention on an important element of the scene or story. The more importance it has, the closer the shot tends to be.

Some filmmakers use this technique as a foreshadowing tool. Maybe in the beginning of the scene you choose to show a close-up of a tool set. Why? It seems very random. Well, in film nothing should be random, and experienced viewers know this. Maybe five minutes into the scene one of the characters needs to pick a lock, so he grabs a very small screwdriver. Aha! Here's why you showed the tool set in the beginning of the scene. When the character starts to fuss about picking the lock, the viewers will say to themselves, "Maybe he should look in that tool set." If you don't show the tool set, and all of a sudden your character randomly stumbles upon it at the most convenient moment, then your viewers may mumble, "How convenient" or "How did that get there?" That takes them out of the story.

FIGURE 2.19 This wide shot shows a group of characters in the middle of a scene. At this point, the emotions have been established. To draw the viewer's attention to empathize with one character, the next shot should be a close-up.

FIGURE 2.20 This close-up shot follows the wide shot shown in Figure 2.19. It isolates this character and his emotions from the rest of the group. By ordering your shot selection this way, the viewers will focus attention on this one character and forget about how the other characters feel.

The trick is that, in both situations, the tool set *is* completely random, convenient, and borderline unrealistic. But when you prime the viewers to integrate the tool set in their minds, for some reason it no longer feels random. By showing a simple shot in the establishing of your scene, it changes the viewing experience from unbelievable to believable anticipation.

REINFORCING THE CONFLICT

Remember that shot selection subconsciously leads viewers to interpret conflict the way you want them to interpret it. Let's go back to the beginning of Chapter 1:

- Every story arc has a conflict.

- Every scene has its own arc.

- Multiple conflicts can be happening simultaneously.

- It's all about the main character's perception of conflict.

Let these four facts guide your shot selection. It's not the law, but a guideline. For example, say you have a scene in which two women are racing up a mountain, and the first one to make it gets a thousand dollars. They're also best friends, and their husbands are good friends as well. While climbing up the mountain, there is a good bit of conversation about their husbands, the friendship between them, the race up the mountain, and the idea that they are pretty scared of falling off the mountain.

To be a good editor, you need to be a good listener. Listen to the narrative in the scene. From the text alone we determine that this is either a relational conflict or a situational conflict. It could be a relational conflict because they're racing for money, and it could be a situational conflict because they're climbing a mountain. To determine which is more prevalent, you need to listen to your characters. Let's say you decide this is a relational conflict, and the focus is on the race between them. Now you must visually reinforce that conflict with your shot selection.

So, when they talk about their husbands, you should *not* use close-ups. Instead, choose wide shots during that part of the conversation so the viewers are distracted by the overall scene. There is less emotion during the wide shot. It may even lead the viewers to think about the overall race between the women and ignore the relatively meaningless dialogue.

When they talk about the race—or stop talking completely and focus on the race itself—then it's time for close-ups. The close-ups draw the viewers in and force them to feel the emotion during the important times of the narrative.

When the characters talk about the frightening idea of climbing the mountain, you might use medium shots. Yes, that conflict is present, but it's not as important as the relational conflict.

Listen to what the narrative is telling you about the conflict and make your shot selections based on what the characters are saying. Again, use this as a guideline to shot selection—it's not the law.

B-Roll

There is an A-roll (your main footage) and a B-roll (your secondary footage). *B-roll* has come to mean *pretty footage with no purpose*. It's true that all the footage you use should have some meaning or purpose in the story. Having said that, situations arise that force you to use a meaningless shot in order to overcome a mistake. Maybe you want to remove a line from the middle of an actor's speech. You may want to cut to a shot of the clock in the room. That would be an example of using your B-roll.

Other uses for B-roll include detail shots of the setting, establishing secondary characters' emotions or positions in the scene, or cutaways that advance the story. In any event, B-roll should never be used to show off your skills as a cinematographer for no justified reason.

Connecting Conflict and Shot Selection

Shot selection is a direct result of conflict. It's not the only result, and many things can influence which shot you choose to show. As mentioned earlier, however, the first question you should ask is: "What is the conflict?"

Example Scene of Relational Conflict

Consider a relational conflict—a conflict between two characters in the story. The trick here is that, usually, those two characters are not the only two characters in the story. Let's say there are eight characters in the scene. (Remember, each scene is its own mini-story, and conflict can change from scene to scene while feeding the bigger conflict/arc.) All eight characters are important to the story, but in this particular scene only two are important. The protagonist and the antagonist have a relational conflict. How do we determine that? Remember, it's all about the main character's perception of the moment.

The main character will tell you what the conflict is in the scene. Now, here is how you build this moment:

1. Establish the setting and all the characters by starting with a wide shot or a series of wide shots.

2. From the wide shot showing the eight characters, single out who's important, in order of importance. First, use a medium shot of the protagonist and a medium shot of the antagonist. A series of medium shots of these characters isolates them from the other characters. In essence, you are trying to make the audience forget about the other characters for the time being. Once you show a few medium shots of each, you should be well into the rising action of this scene.

> **OUT OF ORDER MOVIE** *At timecode 1:26:49 is the beginning of a scene that follows a similar pattern to the one just mentioned. It's a relational conflict between Paul, the protagonist, and Brice, the antagonist. Four other characters are present. Watch how seldom any other character is shown during this long scene. As the editor, I force you to focus on Brice and Paul so much that you almost forget the other characters are there during the intense parts of the scene.*

3. It's time to start building emotion and steering the viewers in the direction of which character to empathize with. Contrast the two characters with close-ups of the protagonist and medium shots of the antagonist. That allows the viewers to focus their emotions on the protagonist and prevents them from getting close enough to empathize with the antagonist.

4. After a series of back-and-forth close-ups of the protagonist and medium shots of the antagonist, it's time to present the actual conflict. In a relational conflict, the antagonist *is* the conflict. In a relational conflict, it's a good idea to wait to show a close-up of the antagonist until the antagonist initiates the actual conflict. At this point, the viewers should already be on the side of the protagonist. Holding out on showing a close-up of the antagonist makes this moment of conflict all the more dramatic. It's important to wait until the moment of conflict before showing a close-up of the antagonist because, if you do it too early, the viewers may end up empathizing with the antagonist. And once viewers attach themselves to a character, it's much harder to switch their emotions to someone else in the story.

What about the other six characters? As mentioned earlier, multiple conflicts can be happening simultaneously. If another conflict *of less importance* presents itself during the scene, you can do one of two things. First, you can pull out to a wide shot to diminish the emotion in the scene at that particular moment. But be careful, because doing it at the wrong time can have a negative effect on the emotion of the scene. In this particular case, it would lessen the emotion at a time when a secondary conflict is being presented. (Remember: See through the eyes of the main character.) The wide shot reminds the viewers of the context and allows them to re-establish context in their minds. It reminds the viewers of the other characters in the scene and removes attention from the two main characters while they talk about a conflict that is not driving the scene. (Multiple conflicts can happen simultaneously, yes, but there can be only one conflict with the title of *most important*.)

A second option is to not show a wide shot but a series of medium shots of the other characters. Doing that allows the viewers to focus on the other characters' emotions individually. The two options accomplish the same goal: taking visual attention away from the main characters at a key moment while the story still moves forward.

Example Scene of Social Conflict

Now, let's say you have this exact same setup, only the conflict is the social kind—human versus group. The scene would be edited very differently. Instead of starting out the scene with a wide shot, I may start with a series of close-up establishing shots. I would establish characters and things of relevance in the room before I present the wide shots. This is because there are going to be many more significant wide shots used during a social conflict—in order to drive home the concept of *group.*

The tricky thing here is to not overuse the wide shot. Its lack of connection to specific characters and emotions will inhibit the scene from reaching its emotional potential. Instead, carefully use the wide shots to remind the viewers of the idea of the group during key parts of the scene. Pick moments when the intensity takes a break. Another major difference here is that the protagonist is one person, whereas the antagonist may be the group of seven others. The scene is built similarly to the relational conflict in that it still creates contrast between the protagonist and the antagonist(s). In this particular situation, you have the freedom to choose which character(s) to focus on. Usually, the choice will be based on what they say and do. In a social conflict, everyone should be established and all their emotions should be focused on.

Example Scene of Inner Conflict

It can be tough to show inner conflict, but using symbolic shots makes it much easier. Inner conflict is the hardest conflict to illustrate as the editor. You are trying to translate the characters' feelings to the viewer. Having shots of characters looking into mirrors or sitting and reflecting near a window or a fireplace—anything that represents a character's internal battle—makes inner conflict much easier to establish.

The rules for wide, medium, and close-up shots still apply here in terms of when to use them. With a scene showing inner conflict, one difference is the timing of the close-up usage and its purpose. Say you have the same eight characters in the same room. The frequency of showing the main character goes up dramatically when you're dealing with an inner conflict. Close-ups of the protagonist may happen not just at the most emotional moments, but while the other characters are speaking their lines, for example. The audience stays zeroed in on the main character while someone else is talking. Visually, the scene is *ignoring* the other characters in the room. Of course, the viewers can hear what the other characters are saying, but their eyes have no choice but to focus on the main character's reaction to what is being said.

Each conflict presents its own set of circumstances, and no two situations are alike. The key is to focus on the main character's perception of conflict, and then steer the viewer's emotion and attention to the place that best advances the story and the particular type of conflict that's driving it. That may mean showing a shot the viewers can empathize with—or showing something the viewers have zero connection with, because you don't *want* them to connect in that particular moment.

Other Elements Affecting Shot Selection

The type of project, including the length of the story, and the order in which shots are placed also affect shot selection.

LENGTH OF STORY

How much time do you have to tell your story? A classic comparison is television vs. film. Movies tend to show a lot more close-ups than television. A movie has 90 minutes, give or take, to tell a story and get you to connect with it. A TV show may have seasons upon seasons to do the same thing. Television shows are almost forced to pace themselves in how they connect with their viewers. Creating a story over that much time is a complex puzzle. Great shows that constantly win Emmys—such as *Breaking Bad*, *The Wire*, *Homeland*, and *Mad Men*—are very selective with their close-up shots.

I noted one 45-minute *Breaking Bad* episode that contained fewer than five close-ups. TV shows are always about the big picture. They may be starting to look more like movies, but the infrequency of close-ups remains the same.

The rule is fairly simple: The more time you have, the less urgency there is to develop extreme emotion, and the fewer close-ups you need. Short films, wedding videos, commercials, and so on feel the pressure of time to develop characters and arc quickly. It's imperative for these films to force the viewers to connect with the characters almost immediately if they are going to retain an audience. In a shorter film, you want to draw the audience in with close-ups early on so they have no choice but to connect with the characters. Always assume that people *will* connect with the characters and not turn the film off (always an option). I often start event films, wedding videos, and short films with a series of close-up shots, one after the other, to intrigue the viewer. This way, when it comes to the wide shots, they'll already have the details. This is covered in more detail in Chapter 3.

ORDER OF SHOTS

The way you choose to order shots is an entirely separate discussion that involves narrative perspective. I explore this in Chapter 3. Before going on to the next chapter, check out *The Aviator,* edited by Thelma Schoomaker. The film is a masterful execution of the connection between conflict and shot selection. Many conflicts are apparent in this film, but inner conflict rises above all. Watching *The Aviator* and studying when close-up shots are used is a great exercise in how to connect shot selection and conflict.

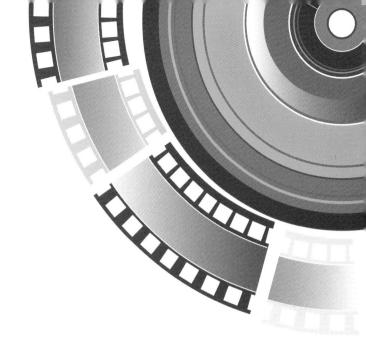

CHAPTER 3

Ordering Clips and Scenes

The ordering of clips is an interesting phenomenon. At times, the order in which you arrange shots and scenes is obvious or dictated for you. At other times, what seems like an obvious order can change while you're in the middle of editing. This has to do with story translation. *Story translation* is what happens when the words on paper get turned into film clips and the clips are arranged into the final film. Each time the story goes to a different medium, a translation happens. Sometimes, things get lost in translation and have to be presented in a different way to get the story across in the clearest way possible.

This chapter explores the little details that make up the *narrative perspective* (the point of view in which the story, or scene, is told from). In addition, this chapter looks at *nonlinear storytelling* (telling a story in a different order that doesn't follow the conventional beginning to end) from an editor's perspective. When it comes to scripting an idea, or mapping out an idea and executing it, a certain translation process occurs. From your brain to paper, from paper to footage, and from footage to final film, things get lost or changed during that translation. What seems, in your mind, the greatest idea since sliced toast may turn out to be not worth writing home about.

Don't worry! This will happen a lot. The ideas in your head will always come out looking and feeling different on the other end, no matter how much experience you have or how good a storyteller you are. The trick is not to eliminate changes in the idea or the feel of the idea—the key to mastering story translation is to anticipate how the story will be different once it goes through all its different phases.

The story translation process is a beautiful element of filmmaking. Think about it. We see the world in real time, with real emotions and real people. We take our human experiences and our interpretations of them and try to fabricate a story with an arc, conflict, and the many other elements that make up a story. All people perceive the world a little differently, and their interpretations are based entirely on their own experiences.

For example, when you read the word "fear," what happens? You see the word, process it, and then the thought travels through your brain and accesses your experiences of fear and you subconsciously understand the word. That's what happens. Here's the glitch in that process: The word fear means nothing without your actual feelings of the fear. If you have no personal experiences to associate with fear, then how in the world can I trust that you understand the meaning of the word? I'm afraid of bugs. Embarrassing, yes, but frightening nonetheless. Some people have zero fear of bugs. If I watch a film with a scene of a spider crawling up the leg of the main character, I would actually rub my own leg just to be sure. Others might watch that scene and not flinch.

A story is the way we explain the world to ourselves. This is where the techniques of film editing come into play. Maybe that same scene with the spider ends up putting our main character in the hospital with a brutal infection. Instead of just showing the spider crawling up a woman's leg and then showing the results in the next scene, maybe I want to show the results first. Then the scene with the spider will strike greater fear in the audience because the fear is now associated with the results of the spider and not the spider itself.

By simply rearranging the presentation of events, I can change the viewing experience and touch a broader audience. This is why the ordering of shots and scenes is a very important element in film editing.

> **NOTE** *Sometimes, stories need to be told out of order. What seems like a coherent story in your mind—following the conventional format of beginning to end—may not achieve maximum emotional potential or even make sense when the film is constructed. It doesn't mean your story or idea is a failure. It means you should think about each scene as its own piece in a puzzle. Moving the puzzle piece (the scene) to a different spot might make things work better.*

There are a million ways to tell your story in an out-of-order or nonlinear fashion, and I want to show you a few ways that I like to do it.

▶ USING A VEHICLE

Think about a movie like *Forrest Gump*. The movie is told by a guy who is sitting on bench and talking to whoever will listen. I like to call this storytelling technique the *vehicle,* meaning using a constant story to navigate your way through time. This movie is broken up by the scenes of Forrest talking on the bench. Imagine watching the story of his life in sequence, and then watching the scenes of him talking on the bench in order. That would make for a very boring film. Instead, the filmmakers break up the scenes on the bench and scatter them throughout the movie. Of course, the *Forrest Gump* script was written this way, but that's not always the case.

The Narrative Perspective: Point of View

There are three narrative perspectives, or points of view, which you probably learned about in high school:

- First-person (the narrator took part in the story)
- Second-person (the narrator is telling a story about the listener, perhaps in a letter—this point of view is rarely used)
- Third-person (the narrator, who may or may not be omniscient, is telling a story that happened to other people, not the narrator)

In filmmaking, point of view is communicated through the order of clips. The order in which shots are presented changes what the viewer knows and when the viewer knows it.

It's very important to know what perspective the story or scene is being told from so that you, as the editor, can give the viewer the correct experience. Narrative perspective also affects shot selection (more on that later in this chapter).

One great thing about film editing is that a story may be intended to be told from one perspective, but that perspective can be changed in editing by simply reordering certain clips. And take note: The narrative perspective can, and usually does, change throughout a story. Each scene should be looked at differently when it comes to the narrative perspective—all while keeping in mind the bigger arc, which also has its own narrative perspective.

The overall story is from the point of view of someone, or many someones. You can tell a story from character A's perspective from start to finish. That doesn't mean that a few scenes within that story can't be told from character B's perspective. You want to know what perspective the story is told from, but be aware that when you dive deeper into a scene or moment, that perspective can change. Don't assume that because your story is told from one perspective that every single moment must be told from that same perspective. In fact, that's almost never the case.

FIRST-PERSON NARRATIVE

In film, the first-person narrative is when the story is told from the perspective of one character at a time. Examples of films with first-person narrative include:

Fight Club: The film is told from the perspective of the character known as Jack

The Matrix: The film is told from the perspective of Neo.

Goodfellas: The film is told from the perspective of Henry Hill.

For a film with voiceover narration, the character refers to himself as "I," or if part of a group, as "we," as in the first example, *Fight Club*. To make a story first-person narrative, voiceover narration isn't required—in fact, narration is never required in any story.

When it comes to interpreting the first-person narrative on the editing board, you want to always be aware of—and even obsessive about—telling the story from a specific character's perspective. This means that the viewer *is* that character. The viewer should know information when the character knows information. The viewer should be unaware of the same things the character is unaware of. If the character walks into a room for the very first time, it needs to be the viewer's first time in that room as well.

OUT OF ORDER MOVIE *Go to 39:12 in* Out of Order *(see this book's introduction for details on downloading the movie). This is the scene right after Paul presents his software to the team of executives and now is in a meeting with the boss (**FIGURE 3.1**). It's a great example of the first-person narrative because we have no idea what will happen. Both the viewer and Paul think he's there for a job interview, but this is not the case. If we knew the intentions of John, this would be a third-person narrative.*

FIGURE 3.1 In this clip from the movie *Out of Order,* Paul is confused when the boss, John, tells him they are not hiring. Because this is a first-person narrative, the viewers know the same things Paul knows—and are therefore confused as well.

You should be able to see how tying the character's knowledge to the viewers' knowledge affects shot selection. Establishing shots become all the more important, yet are dictated by the character's observation. If a character looks at the clock on the wall, you need to show the clock on the wall, and now the viewer is looking at the clock, too. You're not just establishing that there is a clock on the wall—you're establishing the time and the fact the character is paying attention to the element of time. Time may be a factor in that particular scene. Making the viewers aware of time gives them the same feeling the main character has. When thinking about shot selection, you always want to ask yourself, "Which narrative perspective is this scene being told from?" That will help you further narrow down which shots to pick and when to use them.

Ordering your clips on the editing board becomes the deciding factor of what your narrative perspective will be. If a character is walking down a dark, eerie hallway, and he gets to the end of the hallway and something pops out and scares the life out of him and you, that's first person. But let's say you have that same hallway, but this time you reveal what's at the end of it *before* the character gets there—then it's no longer a first-person narrative. It's not a mistake to reveal what's at the end of the hallway, but it does make for a different viewing experience. When the viewers are in the dark about what's at the end of the hallway, then it's almost like the viewers are creeping down the hallway. When the viewers do know, then they are watching and hoping for the main character's safety. That's not the same thing. Depending on the emotion you want your viewers to feel, either one works—but only one is a first-person narrative. With one simple shot in a different spot, you can completely change the narrative perspective.

> **NOTE** If the audience knows something that the main character does not know, it's no longer a first-person narrative.

The general rule with first-person is the viewer *rides along* with the main character. They should uncover the same information along with the main character. The viewer should relate to or empathize with the main character, if not take on the main character's opinions and belief systems.

SECOND-PERSON NARRATIVE

The second-person narrative is a bridge you will not cross many times in your filmmaking career—unless you're making commercials. In commercial filmmaking, the second-person narrative is the most common narrative perspective. The reason commercials use second-person narrative so often is because they include a call to action at the end. The second-person narrative makes the viewer a part of the story, and the commercial wants you to buy a product. In fact, the commercial actually requires you to buy the product to complete the arc of the story. If you choose to not buy the product, it's the exact same thing as turning off a movie before the resolution.

There are many ways to create second-person narrative. Think about music. I challenge you to find a song with lyrics that does not have the word "you" in it. Songs speak directly to the listener. In film, one way to do this is to have a character *break the fourth wall*. Breaking the fourth wall is when a character looks directly at the camera, breaking the fictional illusion and addressing the audience. That second point is very important. When a camera angle goes into the first-person viewpoint of a character, and then characters start looking at the camera, that's not a second-person narrative, and it's not breaking the fourth wall. The fourth wall is broken only when the character *intends* to talk to or include the audience, hence making them a part of the story. Obviously that's an uncommon practice in film. Even in a documentary, people being interviewed tend to look off camera, across negative space, not *at* the camera. That negative space represents the interviewer, whether or not the interviewer appears on camera. Looking *at* the camera is more of an advertisement or a call to action.

Breaking the fourth wall is not the only way to create a second-person narrative. If the voiceover narrator says the word "you" in reference to the viewer, that can be considered a second-person narrative. Again, that's uncommon practice, but it does happen. Take a look at the popular Netflix series *House of Cards*. Kevin Spacey plays a scheming political figure, and the narration involves him looking at the camera and talking directly to the audience. This is very uncommon. He's not just breaking the fourth wall and talking to the camera—he actually references the viewer a good amount. He treats you, the viewer, as if you are his friend in the room no one can see. This show is not the first to pull this off. Shakespeare wrote plays with this very same tactic.

As mentioned, commercials tend to follow a second-person narrative perspective because they are selling something or they require action from viewers to complete their arc. The majority of commercials are trying to sell something to the viewers, which makes perfect sense. But the viewers' inclusion in the story is where things get tricky. Yet again, it comes down to the arc. When you watch a car commercial, chances are you're seeing every part of the arc with the exception of the resolution. Why? Not including the resolution gives the story an incomplete feeling. This is done on purpose to draw you in even more. Surely you've watched a commercial and said to yourself, "I want that." Now, if you go buy that product, you've completed the arc and you are a part of the story. Your buying whatever the commercial is selling is how the arc completes itself.

Including the viewers in the story gives them a part in the story. Don't confuse this with the first-person *ride-along* tactic. The second person is very different. The audience has a choice. In the first-person narrative, the audience doesn't have choice—they're simply locked into a singular character, and whatever that character does or feels is supposed to project onto the viewer. In the second person, that's not the case. Public Service Announcement (PSA) commercials are great examples. They usually break the fourth wall and require the audience to take action. They may ask for a charitable donation or ask the viewers to call a toll-free number. The audience then has a choice whether or not to take action. If they do, the goal has been accomplished, and the story is completed. If they don't, the story stops right there and never completes. If we turn that same situation into a first-person narrative by adding a character for the PSA to address, the viewers no longer have a choice about whether or not to contribute. Instead, viewers must accept the decision of the character they are experiencing the story from. Therein lies the major difference between first- and second-person narratives.

THIRD-PERSON NARRATIVE

The third-person narrative is the most common narrative perspective in filmmaking, especially in movies, television, or pretty much anything that's not a commercial. This is when the audience is simply a passive observer. Let's go back to that dark, eerie hallway mentioned in the discussion about first-person narrative. Maybe you want to show the audience what's at the other end of the hallway in hopes of giving them a different viewing experience. Now you're in a third-person narrative. The audience knows something the main character doesn't.

Using a third-person narrative produces entirely different emotions. Instead of uncovering the mysteries of that hallway in real time with the main character, viewers already know what they'll find at the end. Now it becomes about the main character's reaction. It becomes about rooting for that character. You're cheering her on. Maybe you talk to the screen and say, "No don't do it!" This is called the *God effect*. You know things the main characters don't know, or you know them before they know. Anticipation still exists, but the anticipation gets shifted from asking "What's going to happen?" to "I can't believe the main character is about to find out what just happened." We see this all the time in television shows with many different characters and storylines. We watch as passive observers. We are not watching from any one particular character's perspective.

> **TIP** *In editing, the narrative perspective boils down to what order the audience receives information in. It's as simple as changing the order of shots and storylines.*

Keep in mind that the narrative perspective can change from scene to scene. It comes back to the example of the dark hallway; you can show the viewer what is at the end of the hallway before the character walks down the hallway. This would make the scene a third-person narrative, even if it wasn't intended that way. But that doesn't mean every scene is told from this perspective. It's also important to understand that the editor can change the narrative perspective by simply changing the order of clips. Just because a scene was written and intended as a first-person narrative, it doesn't mean the editor can't change it by moving a clip to a different spot. When you start to change the order of clips, in most cases it affects the way the story is told. Stories told out of order tend to be tricky with regard to the narrative perspective they're being told from. Telling stories out of order creates audience intrigue and taps into a lot of points discussed in previous chapters about getting the viewer's brain to participate in the process. This brings us to nonlinear storytelling.

Nonlinear Storytelling: Telling Stories Out of Order

As I sit in in my living room, I can't help but take note of a pretty decent-size DVD collection. (I liked to collect. The key word is *liked*, because DVDs are becoming a thing of the past.) Many of the stories in those DVDs are told in linear fashion, and that's OK. I want to be very clear that this section on nonlinear storytelling is not a condemnation of linear storytelling. Many times, a story told in order is just that good—there's no need to reorder the presentation of events to present the story in its most entertaining fashion. The movie *Gravity* does not need to be told in a different order other than linear. It's amazing as is.

Stories do not always need to be told out of order to be intriguing or sophisticated. As we navigate through the many ways to tell a story in nonlinear fashion, understand that telling a story in order is not a bad thing. All stories will have sections or acts that are told in linear fashion. Linear works well most of the time—it relies on the story content and follows the basic principles discussed in this book. Nonlinear comes into play only when you find that the story, or part of the story, doesn't translate the way you intended.

It starts with asking yourself, "How do I want my viewer to feel during this moment?" Let's say, for example, you've made a movie in which the main character's dog dies at the end of the story, and you don't want the viewer to feel depressed when the film is over. First of all, good luck, because there is no better way to turn your audience against you than to have a dog die in the story. But if you don't want the story to be about the death of the dog, then show me the dog dying in the beginning. Give your ending away first. That way, the dog's death is over and the story turns into something else. Maybe you have a deep life lesson or something you want to get across about the bond between man and dog. If the dog dies at the end, that's all viewers remember. But if the dog dies in the beginning, then viewers have no choice but to take something else away from the film. This decision can be made in editing.

Why to Tell a Story Out of Order

Nonlinear storytelling is where the art and approach to storytelling through editing really relies on the interpretation of the story and filmmaker. Understanding things such as the plot arc, narrative perspective, and other concepts discussed so far are important here in hopes that you don't cross too far over the line of what makes sense. What that means is that you shouldn't rearrange a story to be nonlinear just because. You need a reason for doing so that improves the story.

First, let's look at the reasons and applications for telling stories out of order. You may decide to tell a story out of order before filming, or you may make the decision on the editing board. Either way works. My guess is the birth of nonlinear storytelling was an afterthought. Creation comes out of imperfection. Story translation doesn't always work. The idea in your mind won't be exactly what comes out on the other side in the final film. Rather than reordering a story to achieve your original vision of the story, you might change the order to achieve the emotional response you initially wanted from the viewer. Think about it: If you've ever made a wedding film, event film, or anything that is unscripted and you are capturing reality, you've already done this. You film all of these events in order, and then you take the pieces you want and assemble them into the desired film in editing. In a scripted film, if a scene is written out of order, you still film it in order to save production time and money. Changing the order of a story or scene in postproduction doesn't change the information the viewer gets—it changes the way in which they get that information.

The process reflects a simple evolution of a desired audience effect. First, you have an idea, and then you execute your idea. After your idea is executed, you sit back, judge, and determine whether it falls short of your original vision. Then you reimagine the idea using the conceit pieces you have, as opposed to using the abstract *what ifs* from before you filmed anything. Now you can look at footage and definitely say what works and what doesn't. You can then ask yourself about the audience response to the certain plot plots. Then, and only then, can you determine whether a certain plot point would work better coming at a different point in the arc. That's the major misconception about nonlinear storytelling.

THE ARC IS CONSTANT

When considering nonlinear storytelling, remember that you *cannot* rearrange the arc. The arc is the constant. If you move the ending of your story to the beginning, you didn't rearrange the arc. Instead, the ending is now placed at the beginning. The arc is locked. Think of it as placeholders for parts of the story. If you place an event in the beginning, it's now part of the beginning. That's why you should be careful about rearranging the story. The film *Fight Club* starts with a scene from the ending. That's a nonlinear approach. That piece of the ending gives part of the ending away, but not the part that matters. The piece of the film that is placed in the beginning is now *part of* the beginning. The storyteller believed we needed that information in order to continue with the story.

Sometimes certain plot points are better positioned at a different point in the arc. It all comes down to the basic understanding of the arc, as discussed in Chapter 1. In the beginning of a story, it's important to establish the setting, mood, and conditions that exist. And it's important to get the viewer to participate in the process and start asking questions. Once viewers ask questions, you own them.

Taking a plot point from the middle and moving it to the beginning—such as in the movie *Goodfellas,* which opens with a scene from the middle of the film when they're driving to go dig up a body—is naturally going to spark questions. Only the questions are different and more extreme. If a story is told *in order*, simple questions are asked, such as "Who is that?" and "How are they connected?" If you move the ending to the beginning, the questions are more like, "How does the story get here?" It's very important to understand the participatory difference between the questions.

- The question "Who is that?" is usually answered quickly—and it needs to be. The linear approach relies on getting the viewer to ask many questions and get many answers.

- The question "How does the story get here?" isn't answered until the end of the story. It's a lingering question that occupies the viewers for the duration of the story. It becomes the story's driving force. From the moment viewers ask themselves such a question, they'll try to feed that question with everything they see—very much like a mystery.

Thinking of stories this way dramatically changes the viewing experience. There is no better way—or worse way—to tell a story. Neither technique is more or less effective. There is no magic bullet point to determine which out-of-order storytelling method works best. Everything is situational.

Let's break down the situations, the applications, and the viewers' reactions when you decide to tell a story out of order.

Intercutting

Intercutting is when you cut back and forth between two different scenes. Say you have two scenes, back to back, and the second scene is a recap of the first scene.

> **OUT OF ORDER MOVIE** *For an example of intercutting, see timecode 03:20 in the* Out of Order *movie and watch the first flashback scenes with the group on a bench (**FIGURE 3.2**). The scenes on the bench were all filmed at the same time and intended to run straight through without cutting back to the interview. It seems as though it was intended to intercut, but it wasn't. Fortunately, it works well. This keeps the viewers on their toes because we never stay in one scene too long.*

FIGURE 3.2 The flashback scenes filmed on a bench in *Out of Order* are examples of intercutting.

INTERCUTTING AND FLASHBACKS

Let's say that in the first scene of a movie, a girl is being interrogated by FBI agents as a possible murder suspect. This scene is a third-person narrative. That means the viewers know who the actual murderer is but the character does not. The murderer happens to be her boyfriend. The interview goes on, and the questions are pretty basic: "What was your relationship with this person? Where were you on this particular evening? Would you have any reason to wish harm on the victim?" As the interview winds down and the agents seem to be getting nowhere, they ask if anyone other than her has been in contact with the victim in the last month. She says, "No, just me and my boyfriend." The boyfriend part piques the FBI's interest, and they write down his name. The significance of this is meaningless to the character, but not to the viewers. We know her boyfriend is the killer, and now the FBI has his name on a piece of paper. That's a big deal.

Now, in the second scene, the main female character and her boyfriend are in bed together discussing the interview. The boyfriend asks her, without giving away his motives, what they asked her. She says, "Nothing. It was a waste of time. They asked me a bunch of questions I didn't know the answers to." Then she mentions that she gave them his name.

Those are your two scenes. Visually, the FBI interview scene could be intense if filmed correctly. The scene in the bedroom would likely be worthless. Why? We don't learn any new information. There are two choices here. One, you cut the second, which isn't a bad idea. Or you intercut the scenes, with the first scene as a flashback. You take the "worthless" scene in the bedroom and use it to set up what happened with in the FBI. The order would look something like this:

Scene 2_Boyfriend asked how the interview went. She says fine, and then says they kept asking stupid questions.

Scene 1_FBI asks female character a bunch of stupid questions.

Scene 2_They asked me where I was the night of the murder.

Scene 1_FBI asks where she was the night of the murder.

Scene 2_She says they asked if she knows anyone who had come in contact with the victim in the last 30 days. The boyfriend asks what did she say? (You don't reveal the answer here.)

Scene 1_FBI asks if she knows anyone who came in contact with the victim in the last 30 days.

Scene 2_She tells the boyfriend she gave them his name.

Scene 1_Shots of the FBI writing his name down on the paper.

With the intercutting, you have drawn out the anticipation (rising action) and combined two mediocre climaxes into one good one. You are not intercutting simply because you don't want to cut one of the scenes; you do it so you can spend more time in the rising action and capitalize on the anticipation. Note that the scene with the FBI is in the past, and the scene in the bedroom is in the present. Also note that this switches from a third-person narrative to a first-person narrative. Viewers no longer watch the scene with the FBI interview in same way. They now watch from the perspective of the boyfriend. The reveal in the intercut version is the fact that they have the boyfriend's name on a piece of paper. This makes the scene much more intense. You uncover the biggest reveal from the first person point of view.

INTERCUTTING CONCURRENT SCENES

Another very common way to use intercutting is to intercut two scenes that are happening at the exact same time:

> Mary is walking down the sidewalk of First Street.

> Bill is walking toward First Street.

These two scenes cut back and forth until, finally, Mary walks into the street without looking at the oncoming traffic. Bill comes out of nowhere and pulls her out of harm's way. He saves her life, they fall in love...the end.

The goal of a simultaneous intercut is that the scenes are separate until they get to the climax, and then they merge into one scene and share the same climax, falling action, and resolution.

▶ **INTERCUTTING IS NOT TO BE OVERUSED**

Intercutting is best used in moderation. You wouldn't use it from the beginning to the end of a story. It's usually reserved for combining two or more scenes. In shorter length films, intercutting may be more common, but this storytelling technique is best used for moments. You can use intercutting at any point in the story, and sometimes the story remains linear and sometimes not.

INTERCUTTING ORDER

Keep in mind that you should only intercut when two scenes "need each other" to be intriguing. When you do this, in most cases you'll take a beginning from one of the scenes, the rising action and climax from both, one of the falling actions, and one of the resolutions. This is not a rule—it's just a loose guideline. The reason it works out this way is because the rising action and climax can handle being drawn out a little more than the rest of the plot points because they contain more excitement and anticipation.

FILMING FOR INTERCUTTING

You can plan the flashback intercutting style prior to production. This involves thinking ahead and knowing in advance that you're going to intercut two or more scenes. The advantage to knowing in advance that you'll be intercutting is that you have the ability to "film" your own transitions. For example, each time I go to a different scene, maybe I defocus the lens. Then, when I start the new scene, I also start with a defocused lens. I blend the two defocused ends together in editing and it looks like one seamless shot.

Knowing in advance that you will intercut scenes can make the back and forth much more seamless and creative, and the result may feel more natural than if you do it as an afterthought. While it's always nice to know about this in advance, intercutting was born as an afterthought. Many times, two scenes in the story don't work particularly well on their own, and you need to intercut them to make them interesting to the viewers.

Teasers

A *teaser* is a glimpse of something that's either going to happen in the film or that happened before the main action. Teasers are usually presented early on in the film. The goal of the teaser is to intrigue the viewers, set some groundwork for establishing the film's universe, get the audience to ask themselves questions, and hook the viewers.

Using a teaser is a favorite technique of mine, and many filmmakers for that matter. The reason is that it works. It works very well. Think about the goals of the plot arc, and the function of the beginning. Questions are the key, remember? When the viewers ask questions, they are participating in the process. And when the viewers participate in the process, the film is much more entertaining. The teaser is a way to begin a film with a piece of the climax or a scene that's out of context enough to cause disorientation in the viewers' mind.

Sometimes, a teaser never comes back—it's not played again in sequence. Whether it does or doesn't, the teaser disorients the viewer, sets the stage for the tone of the film, and requires audience participation from the opening clip. A teaser that is shown out of order and then played in sequence, though, is slightly more rewarding. It acts as a double climax because it's usually a part of the climax and puts in context everything played up to the point where it plays in sequence. It gives the viewer the "aha" moment you want them to feel. Using a teaser is by far the most common technique used in nonlinear storytelling.

> **TIP** *Using a teaser sets the tone for your story. It's one of the most effective ways to hook viewers, draw them in, and get them to participate in the story.*

UNIVERSE'S SETTING TEASER

Let's begin with the *universe's setting teaser*. I call a film or a story a "universe," whether it's set in the world we live in or in an imaginary world such as *Star Wars*, *The Matrix*, or *Inception*. In those films and others like them, there is a great deal of "catching up" viewers have to do. You need them to understand the rules and laws of your story because they are different than the world the viewer knows. Other times, the universe is based on the world we live in, but the conditions are so severe that we still need to be fed information in order to understand what's going on. When you have a story where the viewer needs a universe's setting teaser, everything from then on consists of the viewers gathering information about your story so that when the climax happens, they understand it. That is how they "catch up."

FLASHBACK TEASERS

Sometimes, a teaser is a scene from the past. The scene plays and then the story fast-forwards to present day. The use of the scene from the past is most likely to establish some type of motivation for a character in the story. It will justify everything that happens in your story. Unlike the most commonly used type of teaser, a teaser from the past will never play again in your story. This brings us to the teaser we know and love.

FLASH-FORWARD TEASERS

The most common way to use a teaser is to take a random scene, usually a piece of the climax, and start your story with it. The viewer then watches everything after the teaser with the mindset of trying to figure out how the story fits into that moment. This is called a *flash-forward teaser*. The viewers will see the teaser scene again, and when they do, it will be very rewarding because it will explain the teaser's meaning and, most likely, give the viewer an "aha" moment.

This is what *Breaking Bad* was so good at doing, even in the very first episode. Among the first images you see is Walter White recording a confession tape and then holding a gun out and pointing it at the oncoming sirens. The obvious conclusion is that he is being caught in illegal activity. Then the story rewinds and we see nerdy Walter White as a high school chemistry teacher. Viewers know they are about to go on a wild journey for the next 47 minutes. The first thought in my head was, "How are they going to get us to this point in that amount of time?" And sure enough, they explained it perfectly.

Vehicles

The *vehicle* is another nonlinear technique used by many filmmakers, especially those making documentaries. The nature of this technique is to use a constant scene to navigate your way through time and the story. Here's an example: Suppose you have a really long interview and loads of footage to support the topics discussed. You construct the story by using the interview footage in the order in which you want to tell the story along with the supporting footage as cutaways to strengthen the overall perception of that story. The best part about a vehicle is that you can think about the constant scene as *narration* and the supporting footage as the secondary story. Think about movies such as *Forrest Gump*, *The Social Network*, *The Curious Case of Benjamin Button*, and *J. Edgar*. What do these movies have in common? They all have a vehicle—a constant scene to navigate their way through time and the story (**FIGURE 3.3**).

OUT OF ORDER MOVIE *The entire* Out of Order *film is told through the vehicle of the interview.*

FIGURE 3.3 In *Out of Order,* the interview provides the vehicle for structuring the story.

When using a vehicle, the story does not need to proceed in order. The interview can discuss events that happened in 1990, and then 2002, and then 1989, in that order. It does not need to follow the standard pattern of time. This is one of the easiest stories to create because you can approach everything that's not the interview as B-roll. The secondary footage is entirely necessary to the story, and it's visual stimulus, but it's not needed to actually tell the story.

The singular goal of the vehicle approach is to take a boring interview, told in order, and chop it up, rearrange it, and put it back together again in a more concise, entertaining arc. Most documentaries and any other docu-style film use this approach. Examples include the movies *Fab 5* and *Cocaine Cowboys,* and the TV show *Cosmos.*

▶ USE VEHICLES WITH CARE

A word of caution about using this approach: It's easy. Maybe too easy. You may default to this style when another approach may work better and be more entertaining. It's simple to think of a story from scratch and gravitate toward the vehicle approach because you're blinded by the high success rate. Just because a story is good and well done upon completion doesn't mean it's the best story it can be. That's an important concept to understand here—and in all nonlinear stories.

A good example of a documentary that doesn't employ a vehicle is *Sicko* by Michael Moore. He uses a more exploratory way of telling his story. It feels like we, as the viewers, are on a journey with him. The film is not told through a vehicle of interviews but rather by him and his cameraman, going from place to place, looking for answers.

The whole idea behind telling a story out of order is that you're not satisfied with the conventional approach and hope to bring it to another level. Explore all options before opting for a vehicle. For filmmakers who specialize in wedding stories or commercial events, using a vehicle is lower on the totem pole than a linear approach. It's much easier to tell a story in the vehicle form than the linear form when there is no script. It's very easy to walk around, get some interviews, and then place B-roll shots on top and call it a film. It's the easy way out. Think deeper about your story. While most of the alternatives will be much harder to create, filmmaking is all about pushing yourself to the next level.

Multiple Stories, Common Plot Point

A film that combines multiple stories with common plot points will be, by far, the most challenging nonlinear story to create. You're now dealing with several stories, usually three, and you need as many arcs as you have stories. The stories may or may not intersect, but they have a common plot point or character that connects them. Think about the films *Crash*, *Babel*, and *21 Grams*. These three films follow multiple stories, but they involve a common trait, theme, character, or plot point that makes them into one big story. The stories can stand alone, or they can be treated as one.

> **TIP** *If you plan to follow multiple stories, the key is to treat each story separately, while keeping your eye on the common link between them.*

When working with multiple stories, editing patterns play a major role in communicating to viewers the subtleties of the story (more on pattern and symmetry in the next chapter). For example, you might only use close-ups when the story concerns the common link between the multiple stories. That tips off the viewers that something important is happening during those scenes. Instead of spoon-feeding your audience the common plot point, you can draw them with the selective use of close-ups.

Telling a story through multiple stories united by a common plot is a seldom-used approach that requires a great deal of advance planning. You can't exactly decide to do it in the editing room, after the fact, and expect the story to become clear to your viewers. If you do decide to complicate things for yourself,

Be sure to construct the separate stories as simply as possible.

know that editing plays a major role in whether your effort is successful or an epic failure. Be sure to construct the separate stories as simply as possible so you don't cause too much confusion for your viewers. There is such a thing as a viewer asking too many questions. Too much of anything is not good.

Telling the Story Backwards

Why would you want to tell a story backwards? Because sometimes, the ending isn't the most exciting part of the story. It comes down to the journey, not the destination. The question then switches from "What?" to "How?" Viewers are asking themselves, "How did these certain plot points come to be?" Telling a story backwards is tricky because you have to rely on the viewers' interest in knowing *how* something in the story came to be as opposed to *what* came to be.

Many successful wedding videos are told backwards because the ending is obvious—the couple gets married. The real question is *how* they got there. In that case, the climax becomes how they met. True stories that are part of public knowledge lean on this storytelling technique a great deal because the ending is widely known. Think of a great sports documentary such as *Survive and Advance*. This is the unlikely tale of the North Carolina State basketball team winning the NCAA men's basketball tournament. The ending is *in* the title. The team survives games and advances. But *how* the team does it is the real story. The end may be public knowledge, but the journey of how they arrived there is not.

When you tell a story backwards, the arc does a flip. The ending becomes the beginning, and the falling action becomes the rising action. The climax usually stays where it us, the rising action becomes the falling action, and the beginning becomes the end. That may sound simple, but it's not as easy as it sounds. When you take an ending or resolution and move it to the beginning, it is now the beginning. It needs to take on the characteristics of the beginning. It needs to introduce characters and have all the other characteristics of an exposition. Just moving the ending to the beginning doesn't achieve the backwards approach. The ending needs to *become* a beginning.

You can tell any story backwards, many times using intercutting as a part of the story. You may need to leave out part of the story, based on where an action falls in the arc. You can save any parts you leave out for later in the story.

> **TIP** Try the backwards method when the ending is (1) common knowledge or (2) not as exciting as originally anticipated. You can easily change to a backwards technique after a film is shot, but know that elements of the story will need to be moved to different parts of the arc with intercutting or even completely ignored.

▶ QUESTIONS TO KEEP ASKING YOURSELF

Ask yourself the following questions, in this order, every time you edit a film:

1. What is the story and how should I place each plot point into the arc?

2. What is the conflict?

3. What perspective is the story told from?

4. How do I want my viewers to feel during this moment of the story?

5. Is there a better way to present this story that makes it clearer or more intense?

I will add questions to this list as we move deeper into more abstract concepts, such as pacing and time. For now, this list is very important. You should know how to answer these questions about your films—or any film. Pick a film off the top of your head and try to answer questions 1, 2, and 3. Questions 4 and 5 apply only to your own stories. If you have a good grasp on how you would answer these questions, you're doing great.

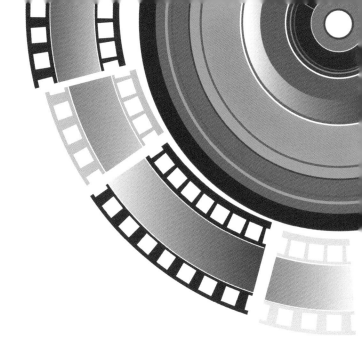

CHAPTER 4

Pacing: Timing and Types of Cuts

One, two, three, four. One, two, three, four. One, two, three, four. One, two, three, four. One, two, three, four. One, two, three, four. By now, maybe you skipped most of that because you couldn't imagine the purpose of it or you thought it must be some kind of mistake. Or, maybe you trusted the book enough to read each number, which allowed a rhythmic pattern to enter your head. The repetition forces you to stop *reading* and start recognizing the shape of the words. It's similar to speed-reading. Your mind forms a flow, and after a few counts you begin to say the phrase, "one, two, three, four," the same way each time.

Mastering pacing is something you should strive for.

Once the flow is formed, it's hard to break unless you give it a different flow. I used the word "rhythmic" earlier. Please note there is a major difference between pacing and rhythm of a film, as I use the terms in this book. Pacing is the timing of cuts, the topic of this chapter. Rhythm is the flow and separation of the overall story, which is covered in Chapter 5.

The purpose of the one, two, three, four count is to show you the foundation of what pacing actually is in a film. The four principles of pacing are:

1. Pattern
2. Symmetry
3. Flow
4. Timing

Pacing is your single most important editing philosophy and is the hardest to grasp. I could sit side by side with you for a year and you still might not master it. The key to pacing is to understand the difference between good pacing and bad pacing. Mastering pacing is something you should strive for, but there will never be a day when it comes to you automatically. At times you may be sharp, and at other times you may be sloppy, but you are generally never going to be perfect.

Defining Pacing

Pacing is an abstract concept that takes practice, practice, and more practice. But don't get frustrated. I'm working on a music video right now and I had to recut it three times until I felt the pacing was right. That's the nature of editing. The important thing is that I knew the first two cuts were not paced well and that the third cut was right. I knew when to keep going—and when to stop. That's what you need to understand about pacing.

The biggest misconception about pacing is that it has anything to do with speed (fast cuts or scenes) or time (length). It's often assumed that the faster something is edited, the better the pacing is. Wrong, wrong, and more degrees of wrong. Something that is cut fast can be perfectly paced. Something that's cut extremely slow can be perfectly paced.

Pacing Examples: Slow and Fast

A lot of great editors believe pacing is managing and utilizing the *space* in a scene—*space* meaning dead air. Some of the greatest examples of pacing come from Quentin Tarantino. The pacing of the conversations in his films really sets the bar for pacing. An example that sticks out in my head is the basement bar scene in *Inglourious Basterds*.

For those who have not seen the film and are planning to, watch it right now because a spoiler is to follow. In the scene, British and American soldiers, who are pretending to be German, meet up with their German contact. She is a famous German actress who is playing a card game with a few Nazi officers when they arrive. When a German character recognizes that one of the British men is not German, the mission falls apart and many people die.

That scene is a masterpiece when it comes to pacing—yet the pacing is very slow. That particular scene manages the space very well. There are long pauses between lines of dialogue and it feels just right. The pacing builds intensity instead of diminishing intensity. Yes, the great writing and acting help, but the editing is a crucial element. In fact, the editing may be the key ingredient to making that scene, and all scenes like it, the masterpiece it is. It comes back to what I said in Chapter 1 about the viewer anticipating what will happen. In this scene in particular, the viewer has a pretty clear understanding of what's going to happen, and the long pauses in the dialogue allow them to relish the anticipation of the predicted outcome.

Pacing ties directly into story arc and conflict. You'll notice in that scene that the back-and-forth dialogue gets *slower* as the scene goes on. What's happening is that the scene gets slower as the outcome becomes clearer. Tarantino uses anticipation as a means to manage the dead air in the scene. The pacing gives you plenty of time to anticipate the many possible outcomes of the scene.

Pacing can—and often does—change. The pacing of a particular scene is for that scene only. Pacing is a situational concept, which is why there are no magic bullet points for getting it right.

A 10-minute dialogue scene in *The Social Network* also takes place in a bar, but it couldn't be more different from the *Inglourious Basterds* scene. In *The Social Network,* it's very fast. And it, too, is a masterful example of the art of pacing. This film, by the way, won the Academy Award for Best Film Editing.

Pacing and Effects on the Viewer

The speed of these two example scenes may be very different—one fast, one slow—but both are paced perfectly. Pacing is situational. It's based on the desired feel, mood, or outcome, and is an ever-changing phenomenon. There is no set rule. It's not as if drama is paced this way and comedy is paced that way. There certainly are trends (which I discuss later), but no rules. A scene may start out fast paced and yet slow down right in the middle.

I have formulated an equation (discussed later in this chapter) that may help you determine the proper pace at any given time. But first, you need to learn the importance of *feeling* the right pace. Most of the time it comes down to feeling and instinct. Consider a heart-rate monitor. Slow indicates tension, fast means intensity or action, and normal means, well, normal.

SLOW PACING

A slow heart rate represents things like tension or anticipation. Beep … beep … beep. Those long spaces give you time to think. What's happening? When will the next beep come? *Will* the next beep come? Relate those beeps to the scene in *Inglourious Basterds* and the dramatic pauses between lines. You have time to anticipate. You have time to let your mind wonder about the possibilities. You can feel the tension in the room.

The slow heart rate can fall on the totally opposite end of the emotional spectrum as well. You can also relate romance to a slow heart rate and rely on the very nature of being in the moment to create that pace. Picture a couple lying in bed with dim lighting. They're laughing, giggling, and talking about their future together. The long spaces between their lines can let you project yourself into their moment, or think of a moment that was similar in your life. The slow pacing is a good calling card for romance because it allows the viewer to really feel what's happening in the scene.

FAST PACING

A fast heart rate represents action or intensity. Beep beep beep beep beep gives you no time to think; you're just perceiving the storyline at an alarming rate. A great action scene or otherwise intense scene should actually raise the viewer's heart rate.

My best friend is a neuroscientist who loves nothing more than a good experiment. We did a little testing of our own and discovered that the way a film is edited has physical effects on the viewer. We found the effects to be most apparent during action sequences. We monitored the heart rate of several subjects in three age groups, all with similar health histories. (Apparently, that matters in a scientific study—which is why I needed my friend or else I would have just used random people.) We had them all watch the same movies in the same environment and noticed a spike in heart rate during the action sequences. The spike was relatively substantial—an average increase in heart rate of 9 percent. It wasn't on the level of a workout, but there was a common spike among them all at the same point in the film. That may not seem like a lot, but if you consider that the subjects were sitting in chairs and not doing any physical activity, it's pretty impressive.

Then we showed them all an action sequence from a different film, out of context, and nothing happened. That suggests that context, or the lead-in, matters for emotional investment. And then we did a third test: We showed one test group an action sequence with poor pacing and we showed another test group the action sequence with perfecting pacing. The results were amazing. The viewers who watched the film with proper pacing had the physical response. The ones who watched the film with improper pacing showed no spike in heart rate whatsoever. It was a fascinating test, and one day I hope to do a real study and publish the data. But for now, my point is this: Pacing affects the viewer physically. And note that the lead-in to scenes also has an effect on how successful certain moments will be.

Pacing affects the viewer physically.

Fast-paced scenes should keep viewers on the edge of their seat. There are different levels of fast. There is fast dialogue cutting, and then there is *car-chase–like* action. Obviously the action sequence with no dialogue, or limited dialogue, will be much faster, but keep the heart rate monitor in your mind. For the sake of argument, let's say that a fast cutting dialogue scene would hit 90 on a heart rate monitor, and an action sequence would range from 120 to 150. (Please note that these rates represent our scaled measurement, not a viewer's actual heart rate. Just know that the viewer's heart will be beating a little faster than normal.)

NORMAL PACING

Normal is the constant in the equation. Normal equals nothing—no drama. Normal is your normal heart rate in everyday life. Normal is you getting dressed. Normal is you eating breakfast. Normal is important because when something not normal occurs, you recognize it. Normal is the gray area between black and white. A good film is normal much of the time. It's the flat parts of the rollercoaster between the ups and downs.

This is why pacing changes all the time. Let's say Jenny is outside working in the garden, minding her own business (normal). We hear a child screaming from inside the house, and Jenny pauses to listen. (At this point, the slow heart rate amplifies the anticipation.) Then the scream happens again, and Jenny runs inside and finds a burglar robbing the house. (Fast heart rate.) That one scene could take you through a spectrum of emotions and heart rates, and the pacing (timing of cuts) should match each part of the scene.

Now that you have a general idea of what pacing is, it's time to break down the principles of pacing.

Principles of Pacing

Remember the four key elements of pacing: pattern, symmetry, flow, and timing. All four elements don't need to be present—or be a focal point of the timing of your cuts—all the time. However, at least one of the four elements must be present in pacing. By the time you finish this chapter, if you watch any movie, trailer, television show, music video, commercial, or even a news story, you should be able to identify one or more of these principles at play in the cutting efforts.

Are all editors working today good? No. Does everything you see on television and the movies work? No. But for the most part, you will see these principles present—and the better the film, the more you'll be able to spot. Depending on the type of film, you'll probably find one element more present than the others. For example, movies rely heavily on timing and flow, whereas music videos are very much a product of pattern and timing. Symmetry is found in movies, but it's a lot harder to spot than timing. Symmetry can take place over a grand scale in a film, while timing happens constantly.

Symmetry is very prominent in great commercials. Can something be properly paced and be missing one of these principles? Yes. But when it comes to these principles, the more the merrier.

Now, let's explore these principles one by one.

Pattern

Pattern is a recurring editing style in a film that mirrors itself in key moments that require close viewer attention. A very basic example of this is the film *Any Given Sunday*. To me, it's one of the best edited films of all time and that is largely because of its pattern. The film is about football and the politics that go with the game. The editor throws the pattern in your face by cutting to a shot of the crowd each time a player forgets about politics and focuses only on the game. The editor then takes that shot of the crowd and *crossfades* it into a similar shot of the crowd from a long time ago—a time where only football mattered, and politics in the game did not. (A crossfade consists of slowly fading two images together; it is discussed in Chapter 5.) It's a *love of the game moment* that draws you in. The editor uses this pattern in key moments in the film, when big plays happen that change the course of the story. That's an extreme example of pattern—a recurring editing style that has its own meaning.

Generally, the use of pattern is rare and hard to recognize, but it can be extremely valuable. Most editors don't consider pattern to be an element of editing. They think it's just a crafty way to make the viewer pay more attention to a particular element of the story. But to me, pattern always exists in editing. The real questions are: "Are you aware of the pattern? and "Are you in control of it?" Or are you merely a creature of habit who can't help but repeat similar editing tendencies throughout the story?

▶ **PATTERN AND STYLE**

Pattern can happen on a small scale or a large scale, and using pattern can help you develop a style. In fact, pattern is branding. Who are you as an editor or filmmaker? I have a pattern. I use the jump cut a lot (cutting to a different frame in the same clip, which is explored later in this chapter). I do it in every film I make without thinking about it. It's just something I do.

EXAMPLE: BREAKING BAD

I discussed *Breaking Bad*'s use of the teaser in its nonlinear story approach in Chapter 3. If you haven't watched *Breaking Bad*, the show began every episode with a teaser. Six successful years of storytelling and captivating an audience, and the teaser was the pattern. The power of this pattern became very evident with the ending of episode 8, which capped the first half of Season 5, Part 1. (Eight episodes aired, and then one year later the next eight aired.) The ending of episode 8 was a flash-forward to the series finale of Season 5, Part 2, which would not air for another year. Well, during that year speculation swirled about the show and how it would end. Just Google *Breaking Bad ending predictions* to see the thousands of blog posts written predicting how it would end (as far as I know, not one of them was right). This was a flash-forward pattern on a grand scale.

EXAMPLE: QUENTIN TARANTINO AND *INGLOURIOUS BASTERDS*

Another example of pattern on a slightly smaller—but still grand—scale is the masterful slow-paced scene in the basement pub in *Inglourious Basterds*. (The director, Quentin Tarantino, has his own patterns as a filmmaker. It doesn't take long to determine you're watching a Tarantino film.) The reason he can get away with this, or any of the long, drawn-out dialogue scenes in his movies, is that we know someone is going to die at the end of the scene. *Inglourious Basterds'* opening scene runs just shy of 20 minutes—the slowest opening scene I've ever experienced. Not many people can get away with showing a guy chopping wood, washing his face, walking inside, waiting for the Germans to show up, and then having a conversation in real time, and keep the audience on the edge of their seat. Tarantino conditioned us from his first film all the way to this film to know something amazing would happen to conclude this insanely slow-paced introduction. He didn't let us down either. It was a slaughter.

If you've seen any of Tarantino's films, you know this as you know the sky is blue. On a grand scale, pattern is storytelling in and of itself.

EXAMPLE: MARTIN SCORSESE

Martin Scorsese is another pattern-oriented filmmaker. His films have the classic look of long takes (long, drawn-out shots that never cut). In every Scorsese movie there's at least one elaborate take that *seems* borderline unachievable by anyone else. It's his signature. He is old school in that his films aren't *overedited* (too many cuts) as a lot of films are in today's digital world. Whenever I see a long Steadicam shot of someone walking through a room with a few hundred extras, I know Scorsese is the brain is behind it.

EXAMPLE: DAVID FINCHER AND *FIGHT CLUB*

Now, there's one filmmaker who has no signature, and that is David Fincher. I think Fincher is the best filmmaker alive, and arguably to ever live. This is because you can't always tell you're watching a Fincher film. Instead, he puts the story above everything and everyone. You can't help but respect that. For everyone else, it seems, the story is secondary to the style. They make the movie, their way, in their vision, and in their style. This is not a knock on everyone else, myself included, but praise for David Fincher for the simple fact that he doesn't repeat himself. If Fincher does have a pattern or style, it's that he focuses heavily on the pattern of the story and film he's making—and not on any overall style or preference. He creates different patterns in each of his films.

Let's talk about Fincher's movie *Fight Club*. I believe it is the greatest movie ever made. The layers go very deep, and so does the pattern. There are so many hidden patterns edited into this film that it took double-digit viewings for me to catch them all. Unless you know the story, you don't know that Edward Norton's character is talking and interacting with himself the entire film. But once you find that out and go back and watch the movie again, that fact is right in your face over and over again. The first and loudest example of that is when Edward Norton is narrating the line "If you woke up in a different time, at a different place, could you wake up as a different person?" Then a shot of Brad Pitt on an electric walkway appears. I'm not sure I noticed this shot at all the first time I watched the film because the walkway is so crowded. But now, that's the answer to the ending.

Pattern is one of the things that make this film what it is. For starters, Brad Pitt's character, Tyler Durden, flashes onscreen in a single frame several times before he appears in the film. This is not in the book *Fight Club*, which the film is adapted from. No, this is an editing decision made to reference Durden's night job as a screen projectionist, where he splices frames of inappropriate images into family films. Showing Durden himself spliced in similarly is nothing short of genius. As Edward Norton's character says, "No one knows they saw it, but they did." Pattern links those two things in the story.

Now, rewinding a bit in that scene, the film explains how Durden does this. At this point, it mentions that movies don't come all on one reel, they come on a few. And Durden's job is to change the reels in the middle of the movie. Edward Norton says, "It's called a changeover, the movie keeps on going, and no one in the audience has any idea." This is interesting because when the reveal happens during the climax of the film, he repeats the line again, and the pattern occurs. What pattern? Well, the pattern of the way he says the line, and the pacing of the scenes and shot selection are identical. It brings home a visual familiarity that gives the viewer a subtle sense of déjà vu, thus enhancing the climax. The same dropout of music happens, and you see the *cigarette burns* referred to in the original scene. The patterns in this film are endless.

Another thing *Fight Club* has a lot of, related to pattern, is symmetry.

Symmetry

Remember Chekhov's gun from Chapter 1? "If you show a gun in chapter 1, it had better fire a shot by chapter 3." That's symmetry. Editing should mirror the story's symmetry and also create its own. In the story arc, the downslope is kind of a mirror image of the upslope. It goes up to the climax, then comes down. That kind of symmetry should go as deep as you can take it into the finest detail in your film.

Remember, each scene is its own arc, too. This means each and every moment in your film is symmetrical, just like the overall story. Another word for symmetry in the context of storytelling is *balance*. You can't have light without darkness. You can't have happiness without sadness. You need to travel from one extreme to the other. The day starts dark, the sun rises in the east, and then sets in the west. What shape does that make? An arc. And during that day the arc can take us on a wild rollercoaster ride. It could rain. It could snow, sleet, or hail. It could be beautiful or gloomy. The options are endless, but balance is inevitable. There is a psychological need for balance in life and in film.

The visual serendipity of having an even balance of wide shots and close-ups has an astounding effect on viewers. This symmetry ensures you achieve the maximum amount of emotional opportunity in each viewer's mind. The wide shots balance the close-ups, and the medium shots are neutral. The more even the scale of that balance, the clearer the emotional goal becomes. Understanding this is controlling it. If you choose to tip the scales in favor of one or the other, you need to be conscious of it and know what you're accomplishing by doing so. Using more close-up shots than wide shots means you're heavily focusing on characters and their emotions. In this case, you're trying to achieve your emotional goals through expression as opposed to action. It's intense. When you favor wide shots, you're making a conscious effort to make the viewers feel as if they're a part of the scene or in the room.

If it seems like I'm explaining shot selection again, I'm not. The point here is what you're accomplishing with specific combinations of shots. First you learn one punch, and then you learn a combo. Everything in editing is intertwined. Concepts bleed onto each other. Shot selection is really about selecting the right shot at the right time; pacing is about the timing of cuts and balancing the types of shots. Symmetry, one of the four principles of pacing, is the bridge between the concepts of shot selection and pacing. (Keep in mind that we haven't even explored the timing of cuts, which is the implementation of pacing. We're still talking about the principles.)

Let's take symmetry even deeper, remaining aware of the arc and starting with the exposition (the beginning). Let's say that when you establish your conditions in the exposition, you use a specific shot combination to introduce a concept. Jenny walks into a bar and tells the bartender about her money problems. To establish this, you approach it in a standard way: You establish the bar with a wide shot, single Jenny out with a medium, and then use the close-up when she delivers the line, "I'm broke." Then Jenny slides a twenty-dollar bill across the bar and asks for a refill. For this shot, you choose an overhead, shooting straight down on the bar, featuring the top of the two characters' heads and the money. Then you punch in close on the twenty-dollar bill. You end with a close-up of Jenny, smiling and saying, "I would spend my last dollar on this drink, I need it so bad." Jenny winks.

Your shot combination and order is crucial here. Later in the story, Jenny starts a business, makes millions, and gets married. Then she gets divorced, loses most of her money, and the movie ends with her depressed at the bar. Guess what happens next? Jenny slides a twenty-dollar bill across the bar and says, "I would spend my last dollar on this drink, I need it so bad." This is where symmetry plays a role in editing. You've conditioned the viewer to see this moment a certain way, so if you present it the same way, it will have a much bigger impact. You want the same shot order and the same shot selection. I will go as far as to say that each shot should be the same duration. Films do this all the time, and you don't even realize it.

Symmetry can happen in all kinds of ways. Repeating music, using color grades on key moments, and adding sound effects are all ways to cue the viewers to think "I've been here before." When the viewers feel something familiar, you should be accounting for that in the pacing. Sometimes a cue can come from other sources, and you may need to use the pace to cue the viewers, which means approaching pacing for the scene that it is in and not with the goal of symmetry in mind. These concepts are explored in later chapters.

> **NOTE** *The key to symmetry is familiarity. When viewers are familiar with a moment as they enter it, you've accomplished a great deal in your story. It means you told them something, they remembered it, and that information helps tell your story later on. That's impactful storytelling and editing. There isn't a story in the world, good or bad, that doesn't have balance. In film, editing is one of the key ways to achieve that symmetry.*

Flow

Ask a random filmmaker for the definition of pacing. The answer is likely to involve some sort of action. The most common response I hear is, "It just moves," while the person snaps his or her fingers. While that is a basic understanding of pacing, what the person is really describing is a small but very important element of pacing called *flow*. It's easier to understand flow when it's faster, but the films that flow the best are slower. And with the slower ones, it's harder to achieve flow.

A great way to learn flow is by editing music videos. If you are just starting out as a filmmaker and haven't done much editing, start editing music videos. This is not because they're the be-all and end-all of film editing, but because editing music videos can teach you some really good habits. It shows you how to cut to the music and integrate that into the editing of a film. It also can teach bad habits. Relying on cutting to the music is a crutch that can cripple your pacing, so be careful when you try to take the music video approach to any other type of narrative. (The exception is a montage, a collection of short shots edited together to condense space, time, and information, discussed in Chapter 5.)

These days, most videos don't have much of a story. It's sad but true. I don't do many of them anymore. When I first started out as an editor, I did a lot of rap videos. They were basic with people rapping to the camera in five or six cool locations. I didn't know any better, and it forced me to be a good editor. In some situations, editing is all you have to make something remotely acceptable. I believe every editor should work on at least three music videos. You can only take them so far, but it's an exercise in flow. Because there's no story, you usually have one speed: fast. So it flows like a river from start to finish with fast cuts all the way through. This can teach you the value of a single frame.

With a story, however, you need to take your flow and move it into storytelling. You also need to understand that a story has many different speeds. Some parts are fast and some parts are slow. Understanding the flow of the *river* is what helps you determine what cutting speed to use. The speed of the actual narrative is a good indicator of cutting speed. Whatever the speed of the story or the arc is, you want to match it. Flow means making hard choices. You may end up cutting redundant lines. You may shorten or lengthen pauses. You may take a facial expression from one part of the scene and move it to a different scene because you want to alter the speed of the cutting. You don't edit a film exactly how it's shot—you trim the fat and beef up the meat.

I compare the ending of scenes or moments to texting. If you're texting a friend back and forth, it could look a little something like this:

You: Hey what r u doing tonight?

Friend: Nothing, u want to get together?

You: Yeah I get off work at 6, happy hour doesn't end until 9, want to go?

Friend: Yeah let's do it, u r buying the first round.

You: OK cool. I'll have the cold beer waiting for u.

Friend: OK

That's a standard conversation. The part that drives me insane is the response "OK." Really? You wasted a whole message on that? That's how you need to treat film flow. If it doesn't move the story forward, cut it. The "OK" contributes nothing to the story. You can make the argument that it's closure to the scene. When it comes to the beginning and ending, try thinking of each scene as a piece of the bigger story. You don't need closure in every scene. A scene can just end before we, as an audience, see it end.

▶ GOODBYES WITH MEANING

My brother, a lawyer, asked me why people never say goodbye at the end of phone conversations on TV. They just hang up. "It's a waste of time to say goodbye. It's much quicker to hang up," I responded. It's as simple as that. Every second is valuable. Every word that isn't accomplishing something is a second your viewer could give up on you. That is why we let the viewer assume the goodbye without showing it.

Saying goodbye, however, can be a major plot point. Maybe a woman is saying goodbye to her father on his deathbed. In that case, it's an emotional goodbye that will stay with the character for the rest of the story. Here, you linger in the moment as long as you can because you're capitalizing on the emotional.

The lesson here is that it's not about the words spoken—it's about the context they're spoken in. A person saying goodbye at the end of a casual phone call doesn't compare to a woman saying goodbye to her father on his deathbed. Even if the words are the same, the context of the moment calls for a different pacing.

> **TIP** *One of the best things you can do as an editor is edit your scenes with this philosophy in mind: Enter in the middle of the scene and leave before it's over.*

When you enter in the middle of the moment, viewers are already playing catch-up. That gives their minds something to do. They're establishing a backstory in their minds with information you're giving them. The same thing works for the ending. Leave before it's over, and the audience gets to infer the ending with the information you gave them. This feeds the idea that the film is a collaboration between filmmaker and viewer.

Don't finalize things. Now, take this with a minor grain of salt. What I mean is every conversation in your story doesn't need to come to a complete close. Watch any movie at random and count the number of scenes that end with some sort of finalizing line (such as OK, goodbye, see you later) or a character walking out of the scene. You won't find many—or any. That's because of flow. The editor made the choice to trim the fat.

Timing

Timing refers to deciding when to make a cut. Timing is the sixth sense of an editor. Knowing exactly at which frame to cut from one clip to the other is learned by experience. Experience is the key to good timing. Being able to say, "I've been here before" is the true measure of greatness. The main problem with that is that you've actually never been there before. You may have been in similar situations, but not the same.

Before becoming a filmmaker, I was a professional poker player. You might be thinking, "Wow, those careers seem vastly different." Yes, they certainly offer different lifestyles, but the mental focus, attention to detail, and importance of past experiences are quite similar. In poker, they say you'll never be in the same situation two times. It's true. The room, the cards, the money at stake, the people in the hand, the time of day, the build-up to that hand—all of those details come into play during any given hand. It's a true ripple effect. It may seem like you've been in this situation before, but it's not the same.

That's true of film as well. You'll never actually be in the same situation twice. All you can do is take each situation for what it's worth and log it into your mental library as to how such situations play out. You'll call upon your mental library in each and every decision you make. Some call that instinct, and sure, instinct plays a role. But history also plays an important role in the decision of when to cut. Being good at pacing doesn't mean being able to sit down with raw footage and make a beautifully paced film on the first try. Pacing is about trial and error. It's about looking at a film and saying, "No, we need to start over." For quick turnarounds, same-day edits, and the like, just know that a rushed film will never reach its true potential. Edited films almost always require a period of mental processing. You shouldn't spend 12 hours editing a film and then immediately judge your work. You need some distance. You need to take time to process.

Pacing is being able to look at a film and know that it's improperly paced. Being a disciplined editor means having the patience to re-edit a film until it feels right. (You'll explore the timing of cuts later in this chapter.)

SPOTTING CUES TO TIMING

When the word "timing" is used in the context of pacing, it's referring to using the cues as a means to cut. *Cues* can come from anywhere, but usually they come from your characters. If a character looks at something, chances are your next shot will be what he sees. It seems like the same idea as the narrative perspective, but the lag time between when the character looks at something and when you show what he sees is timing. How long you delay what the character sees will determine its emotional impact. The cue comes from the moment as well. If she looks into her wallet to see how much money is inside, holding on her face for three seconds before you show the wallet is probably not a good idea because she's just checking. However, if we as the audience know how much money she has, and she's checking her wallet to find out money has been stolen, then you would hold on her face to capture her reaction.

This ties back to the narrative perspective discussed in Chapter 3. When I talked about showing what characters see, I never specifically covered *when* or *if* they should see things.

EXAMPLE: TIMING IN ACTION

Let's say Mary and Sally are sitting in the dining room eating dinner. The story is told from Mary's perspective. Sally asks Mary, "What time is it?" As the editor, you should show Sally asking the question. Then you show Mary looking at her watch. Do you show the actual watch? No. The only reason to show the watch is if the time of day is important to the story. In this case, Mary simply replies, "5:30." Showing the watch would be bad timing.

If several shots of the watch were filmed with the intent of using them, you may feel like you need to show the watch. But don't be distracted by what you have. Why is this a case of timing and not shot selection? Well, it's always a case of shot selection, just as it's always a case of narrative perspective. The pacing will be destroyed if you show the shot of the watch because the viewer doesn't need a visual reference to something that doesn't matter. In short, no matter where you time the shot of the watch, it won't be timed properly. It's a shot set for failure.

Sometimes, editors get lost in the shots they have and feel like they need to use everything. Let's continue the scene. After the time is established, Mary and Sally hear a loud bang in the kitchen. Sally gets up and runs to the kitchen. She looks in the kitchen and says, "Oh no, you're not going to believe this." Mary, walking slowly behind, enters the doorway and sees broken plates on the floor.

The shot sequence and timing would be as follows: You show a shot of the two women reacting to the bang. In the same shot, Sally gets up. You show Sally reacting to what she's seeing in the kitchen, and then her line to Mary. You do *not* show what's in the kitchen at this point. That's bad timing. There are three reason *not* to do that here:

- You've created a moment of anticipation. The viewers are asking themselves, "What is it?"

- The story is told from Mary's perspective; if she hasn't seen it yet, neither have you.

- Once you've seen what made the bang, the story is over. Everything after that doesn't matter.

Now Mary enters the doorway and reacts to what's in the kitchen. Focus on her reaction as long as possible. Then, in the frame before you feel it becomes redundant, cut to what Mary sees. That, in a nutshell, is timing.

Timing of Cuts: The Pacing Formula

Pacing is the timing of cuts. This section helps you determine the proper timing of cuts. Don't confuse this with the concept of timing as discussed earlier. Timing is a singular moment while the timing of cuts refers to a plural concept. This means determining an average cut time through the scene. The equation you're about to learn is not an exact science—it's a guideline to help you analyze the type of pacing you need and analyze whether the pace you've created is correct. Ready? Here it is:

Speed of Conversation + Length of Scene + Number of Characters + Drama + Mood = Pace

Ask yourself, "What's my goal? What's the scene trying to accomplish in terms of feelings of the viewer?"

The following sections discuss these elements of the equation in detail. Remember, each one is only one element of the equation. Each part of the equation plays an equal role in determining what the pace should be.

Speed of Conversation in a Scene

When I say the *speed of conversation,* I'm referring to an actual conversation in a scene. The conversation is the foundation for all of editing, as discussed later. (If a scene doesn't have a conversation, then substitute *scene* for *conversation*, and the scene would center on the unfolding of events.) Even in a music video, the lyrics act as a conversation. The speed of conversation means the natural speed in which characters in the scene communicate back and forth. If the scene is an argument between two characters, it would have a much faster back and forth—faster cutting—than if two characters are talking about the weather. The pacing of the scene reflects the speed of the conversation.

> **OUT OF ORDER MOVIE** *Take a look at timecode 1:15:19 in the* Out of Order *movie. Focus on the pacing of the scene: It starts out slow and builds throughout the scene, and then drops back to a slower pace by the end (**FIGURE 4.1**). It follows the natural flow of the conversation. However, the part you should be focusing on here is that as the speed of the conversation picks up, the cutting speed also picks up.*

FIGURE 4.1 The conversation starts slow and then speeds up.

It's best to look at the natural flow, or intended natural flow, of the conversation and use that as a basis. For example, wedding vows naturally have a slower back and forth. Usually, the vows are used as the climax of a wedding film, so you may want to find ways that the pacing is faster than the organic flow of that conversation. A trick I like to use is moving into an intercutting sequence (see Chapter 3 for more on intercutting). I use footage from other parts of the wedding, making the vows last longer but with faster cuts.

If you didn't want to interrupt the vows, you could simply use a faster cutting speed during the vows. The key is to include reaction shots from the audience in addition to the bride and groom talking. You don't always have to show the person who is talking. Once their vows are covered with B-roll, you can actually change the speed in which they talk by elongating or shortening the pauses between words.

The speed of conversation is always the first element of a scene I consider. The original intention is always the constant. You're either trying to re-create, go faster, or go slower, but the point is the original intention gives you a reference as opposed to working from an abstract idea.

> **TIP** *The speed of the conversation will have an effect on the average cut time. A slow conversation should average fewer cuts per second than a faster conversation.*

Length of Scene

The *length of scene* is another indicator of pace. The following is not a rule, but a guideline: The longer the scene is, the faster the pacing should be to help sustain interest and make things feel shorter than they actually are. Unless your name is Quentin Tarantino, you're not likely to generate interest in a dialogue scene that lasts eight minutes. Generally, the longer the scene, the faster the pace should be.

Consider two guys talking about the weather. How long do you think you can get away with that before your audience turns on you? Forty-five seconds to a minute might be the longest anyone could stand a scene like that. That's not very long, but it goes hand in hand with the speed of conversation theory. If you have two guys talking about the weather, the speed of the conversation is most likely slower, and a 45-second scene matches with the slower pace. Now you should be seeing how the pieces of the equation start to align. With characters arguing, the scene could easily last two to three minutes, and it would require a faster pace.

Let me throw a monkey wrench into this situation, however. Let's say you have a two-minute scene of two characters talking about the weather, and you want it to feel properly paced. What do you do? First, hope this never happens. Second, one thing you can count on is that if a story takes two minutes to talk about the weather, then it's a very important story element. The weather may be affecting the characters' travel plans or even threatening their lives. These things lead to intensity, which in turn leads to a faster pace. That aligns with the length of your scene.

I've yet to make a film where every scripted scene made the final cut of the movie.

You may be thinking, "What if I have a scene with two characters talking about the weather that lasts two minutes and it's not important to the story at all?" Then your solution is easy: Cut the scene. Hard choices need to be made. I've yet to make a film where every scripted scene made the final cut of the movie. Talking about meaningless weather sounds like a great scene to cut.

Number of Characters

The *number of characters* is another important element in the art of pacing. The more characters you have, the more vantage points you have the opportunity to show. It's a game of numbers. If you have two characters in a room talking about the weather, you're pretty limited in what you can show. Because talking about the weather doesn't generally result in an intense, fast conversation, the pacing is going to be slower. But if you have six characters in a room talking about the weather, then all of a sudden the pacing can be amplified.

> **OUT OF ORDER MOVIE** *Take a look at 1:04:44 in the* Out of Order *film. Two people in a room are talking. Immediately following this scene, seven people in a room are talking. Notice how the pacing drastically switches between the two scenes just because of the number of characters (**FIGURE 4.2**). The conversation isn't more intense, and the speed of the conversation hasn't changed. It comes down to more characters and their reactions. Try counting how many times it cuts to a character who isn't talking.*

FIGURE 4.2 More characters leads to a faster pace and more cutting.

Think about two people in a room talking about the weather; you'll likely have three usable shots. A wide shot, a two-shot of both characters, and a medium shot of both characters. It's unlikely that you would have a close-up of either character because using close-ups would produce a repetitive-looking scene that offers no visual stimulus. If there's no intensity in what the characters are saying, as a viewer I need the visual stimulus of wide and medium shots because the context of the moment is equal to what they're saying.

I have a theory I call "3's company" that says once you add a third person to the scene, you immediately gain an opportunity to show a significant number of shots that you couldn't have before. Let's say you add a third person to the weather conversation scene. Now you still have the original three-shot opportunities, but you also have five more to add to that list. You now have a wide three-shot of all the characters. You have a medium shot of the third character. You also have a combination of two shots showing two of the three characters. This third character offers more shots, which leads to more cuts, which leads to faster cuts, which leads to a faster pace. Here's the best part about the third person: They don't even have to talk. All they have to do is react. If they react to what's being said in the scene, then they're a part of the scene. According to the 3's company theory, the more characters you have, the more vantage points you have an opportunity to show.

Drama and Mood

Drama is associated with what you want the viewers to feel. Drama is something you can control. *Mood*, on the other hand, is something the characters feel, and it's totally out of your hands. (That is up to the story.) These two concepts don't always line up— sometimes they do and sometimes they don't. Think about a comedy, for example. Physical comedy refers to pain. If a character slips and falls in a dramatic way, he's going to feel pain. The viewers won't feel pain, though—they'll just laugh. Drama is between you and the audience; mood is between the characters.

You can have three different characters in a scene who all feel different emotions, while the audience is feeling something different from all the characters. The major thing that comes into play here is the narrative perspective. If you're telling the story from a particular character's perspective, your hands are tied.

Back to the weather conversation. Three characters are in a two-minute scene talking about weather. Two of the characters are joking and the third character is scared. The viewers should associate with the funny characters. Three characters (Number of Characters) + a two-minute scene (Length of Scene) + a fast-talking conversation (Speed of Conversation) + wanting the audience to laugh (Drama) + the mixed emotions of the characters, laughter and fear (Mood) = a faster-paced scene. Almost all the elements point to a fast pace, and the point that brings it home is drama.

> **TIP** Comedy tends to have a faster, poppy pace. It's not quite as fast as action, but it's faster than most genres. (Poppy refers to popcorn cutting, discussed in the next section. It just means that the cutting happens at the ends of lines. Simply put, whenever a character is talking, you can see them. This doesn't mean any genre has a particular cutting style; it's more of a current trend.)

Types of Cuts

Many different types of cuts are available when you hit the editing board. A cut isn't just a cut, unless it's what's known as a hard cut. When choosing the type of cut to use at any given time, your decision will depend on four things: genre, length, style, and pacing. Some genres favor certain types of cuts, which are covered in the following sections.

The thing to remember is that there is never really a right answer. After all, editing is an art form, and you can go in whatever direction you choose. I can only offer guidelines on choosing the types of cuts that follow the pattern of where editing is today. Fifty years ago the trends were much different.

> **TIP** *Pacing will always be your biggest indicator of what cut to use and how to time it.*

HARD CUT

A standard cut, or *hard cut,* means simply cutting from clip A to clip B as shown in **FIGURE 4.3**. You can see here that a hard cut in the middle of this conversation would be seamless. There's no question about where we are. However, if you want to transition to another part in the story, because of the jarring *hard cut* that its name suggests, it doesn't give a viewer much time to acclimate to the new scene. This is why most hard cuts are contained within a scene and not used to go from scene to scene.

FIGURE 4.3 In a hard cut, the most commonly used type of cut, you cut from clip A to clip B.

Hard cuts are quite commonly used, especially in television. Usually, they are used when going from scene to scene. Often a transition isn't needed to make a smooth cut to another moment in your film. The main advantage of hard cutting is that it gives the viewer zero time to process or question.

I always weigh the use of a hard cut based on what I'm trying to achieve in the viewers' response. If I want them to be in moment A, and then instantly be in moment B, I use a hard cut. To make this work, you'll obviously be depending on the audience members to transition themselves to that moment. If you're traveling to a different time in the story, a hard cut isn't a good idea because it's perceived to be the same time period. I discuss the concept of time in Chapter 6.

The exception to this recommendation is if you've established the jumping around in time in advance. In that case, a hard cut is useful because the audience knows instantly where they are and the story moves much faster. Using a hard cut is entirely based on the context.

JUMP CUT

A *jump cut* cuts from a frame in a clip to a later frame in the same clip—or to a clip that looks very similar. The two shots in **FIGURE 4.4** show what a jump cut looks like.

In most cases, I don't recommend jump cuts. If a scene has someone giving a speech on a stage, you wouldn't just cut to a later point in the speech in the same shot. You need to cover the cut with a B-roll shot or cut to a different angle of the speech to keep the visual fluidity. However, at times you can use a jump cut for stylistic purposes. That's something I tend to do quite a bit.

FIGURE 4.4 In this example of a jump cut, the frames look similar because they're from the same exact clip. The image on the right, however, comes from much later in the clip.

In the stylistic format, a jump cut can mean one of two things:

- Passing time
- Repetition over time

Let's start with the idea of passing time. Say that a girl tells a boy, "Wait here. I'll be right back." The girl exits, and the camera fixates on the boy as he waits. The point of your story is that the girl takes forever to come back—or maybe doesn't come back at all. You need to give the viewers the impression of time passing, without forcing them to sit there and watch him wait in real time. This is an ideal time to use a jump cut.

OUT OF ORDER MOVIE At timecode 00:08:04 in the Out of Order *film you can see a great example of a jump-cutting sequence as books stack higher without the frame changing (FIGURE 4.5). This is an example of using jump cutting to pass time in a visually interesting way.*

FIGURE 4.5 Books magically start to stack as the character works.

One way to create this type of jump cut is to lock your camera down and never move it. Then, have your subject run through a variety of actions and poses that are associated with waiting. Maybe he twiddles his thumbs. Then he paces back and forth. He does a few jumping jacks. He stretches. He lies on the ground. You record all that in one long clip, make cut points in the parts you don't want, and then condense the long clip down into its many parts. In the playback, it looks like the subject moves around doing all these different actions, but the shot never moves. This trick gives the audience the impression that a lot of time has passed, but it only took you a small amount of time to do it.

Another way to do a jump cut involves repetition over time. This is the exact same idea, with less need to lock the camera down. Personally, I would still lock it down for seamless purposes, but it's totally acceptable and even trendy to give it a fly-on-the-wall look. Let's say this same boy goes into a clothing store to find an outfit for the big night. You set up your camera over his shoulder as he looks in a mirror and tries on 20 different outfits. You record one long clip and then cut out the dead space. It's the same idea as the other jump cut, except the camera isn't locked down. You might use this same technique in a dialogue setting when a character is doing a repetitive dialogue delivery. Maybe it's a series of jokes or funny faces. The point here is that a character repeats an action in a variety of ways, and you choose to showcase them all, one after the other.

L-CUT AND J-CUT

Editors also need to master *L-cuts* and *J-cuts*. A J-cut occurs when the audio from the next clip is heard before the video. An L-cut is when the video switches before the audio. The names of these cuts come from the shapes they make on the cutting timeline:

- J-cut means you hear the audio before you see the video that matches with that audio. It doesn't mean you're staring at a black screen. It just means you're looking at clip A while hearing the audio from clip B.

- L-cut means you're still hearing the audio from a shot but you're seeing a new shot. The viewer is looking at clip B while still hearing audio from clip A.

Here's an example of a J-cut: A character says his line, and the other character starts to say his line—but the camera remains on the first character. Then, in the middle of the other character's response, it cuts to that second character. The J-cut is the key to creating good conversational dialogue. (Remember, conversations are the foundation for all of editing.)

A good way to practice editing is to take a conversation between two characters and try to edit it together in the most seamless way possible. You can't do that without L-cutting and J-cutting because they make things more conversational. You are accustomed to seeing J-cuts and L-cuts because every drama show on television uses these techniques.

The question isn't really about whether you should be L-cutting or J-cutting—it's about the timing. You can find clues to the timing in the conversation's grammar. When do you cut from one character to the other in a conversation? Listen to the dialogue and try to find the punctuation (such as commas) and beats in what they're saying.

For example, look at this sentence: "I drove to the store, and when I pulled in the parking lot, guess who was standing right there?"

That sentence has two break points delineated by commas. You could use one or both commas as cut points. You might cut once at the first comma, and cut back at the second comma. Doing so offers a conversational flow to the scene and includes the character who is not talking as part of the response. If no natural commas occur in the dialogue, try to find the pauses in the dialogue. Use those moments as your cut points.

Remember these three things:

- For cut points, you can use multiple commas, one comma, or none. If you're cutting to another character during a sentence, use the commas as your reference point for cuts.

- Cutting to the other character's reactions is what adds conversational flow and reminds the audience that this is a conversation. By cutting to an expression, you're creating the conversation. This is why the conversation is the foundation of editing. There doesn't even need to be a response. By simply showing that other character, you have created the response. It's so important to practice this because you do it in editing all the time.

- Not every piece of dialogue offers this opportunity. A character saying "Hello!" does not offer this same technique. You would never want to cut in the middle of a word. That situation is where popcorn cutting comes into play.

All the types of cuts are used in all genres, but drama is where you'll find L-cutting and J-cutting used the most.

POPCORN CUT

Popcorn cutting, which is generally reserved for comedy, is very simple: If a character is talking, they are onscreen. There are no reaction shots while someone else is talking. An extreme version of popcorn cutting is that to show a character's reaction at a key point in the middle of the dialogue, you show the reaction, break the dialogue, and then cut back to the character speaking. Popcorn cutting is also sometimes used in fast-paced dialogue.

Pacing is an ever-changing phenomenon. It changes with the times, and can change right in the middle of a scene. The most important thing is to learn to be able to tell the difference between right pacing and wrong pacing. Once you know that, it's a matter of trial and error.

CUTTING ON THE ACTION

Considering the story arc and conflict are at the top of the list of important things in editing. This is not because they're so utterly important to the actual craft of an editor, but because they're important to the decision making of an editor. It's also because they're overlooked by most editors. Cutting on the action is the single most important technique when it comes to making films *visually seamless*.

The best kind of cut is one the viewers don't see. Of course, you can see every cut, but some you notice and some you don't. Cutting on the action is the best way to hide a cut. *Cutting on the action* is exactly what it sounds like: When action spreads across two or more clips, the editor makes a cut in the middle of that action.

Note that *action* is just another word for *movement*. For example, **FIGURE 4.6** shows a man drinking. Your eyes go directly to the movement (you'll have to imagine the movement in the still image). Always remember that in film: *The viewers' eyes go to movement.* So when viewers watch the completion of an action across two clips, they don't pay attention to the cut.

FIGURE 4.6 Notice how your eyes are drawn to movement—the man drinking. Cutting on the action means making your cut points in the middle of movements such as this.

Here's the best example I can give: Consider a pitcher's wind-up in a baseball game. Say you are filming with two cameras (or maybe one camera and you film the same scene twice). Your ideal cut point is in the middle of the pitcher's release of the ball. As soon as his hand gets to the top of his release, that's when you cut from one clip to the other. The hand motion is happening so fast that your eye is trying to find the finishing of the movement. The searching for movement across clips occurs instantly.

You can use this method on any type of shot. If you have a wide shot of a man setting a glass on a table, you can cut to a close-up of the glass as it hits the table in the middle of the movement. The movement can be fast or slow, big or small. As the editor, try to find the action and use that as a basis for cut points while factoring in everything else, and your cuts will be seamless.

CHAPTER 5

Rhythm
and Time

Rhythm is a concept in film editing that's similar, and often confused with, pacing. So let's get things crystal clear up-front:

- Pacing is the timing of cuts. When do you cut from one clip to the next? That's pacing.

- Rhythm deals with bigger parts of editing that run across the entire story, such as *the separation of scenes, transition between scenes, controlling and managing of time,* and *audience digestion* in or between scenes.

- Time is the time frame in the film. It is an illusion that you control. As an editor, you consider how to speed it up, slow it down, show its passing, and the like.

Rhythm, like pacing, is situational but follows the arc to a degree. I explain how it ties in with the arc later in this chapter.

How I Learned About Rhythm

How to work with rhythm was the first major lesson I learned in film editing. It was the first time I realized how powerful editing really can be. I was making my first film, *Detox.* (I encourage you *not* to look it up because, well, it was my first film.) We were done shooting the movie and in the editing phase. We were working, as a group, on the postproduction, and up to that point we had edited scenes but never put them together. Once we had all the scripted scenes edited, it was time to watch the first rough cut. Keep in mind that I had no formal training and had never made or edited a movie in my life. I was doing it based on instinct alone.

Like all of our editing sessions, we snuck into the University of Delaware library with our fake school IDs to use its state-of-the-art editing suite. We assembled the scenes in order, and I put a simple fade to black between each scene because it seemed like a natural transition for a seamless assembly of the scenes. Then we clicked the Export button and waited—for 16 hours. That's how long it took to export a two-hour film in 2007.

Fast-forward 16 hours later. (Notice how I jumped ahead in time 16 hours? That is an example of rhythm. More on this later.) Now we were watching our first rough cut. I was excited, proud, and having the time of my life.

Two hours after that, I was freaking out. What a piece of crap this film was. I knew it. I'm not one of those artists who are moved by everything they do. If it's trash, I'm the first one to say it. And this was a massive pile of trash. It had no flow, it was too choppy, too long, too boring, and something about it was just…wrong. I was almost in tears. Scott, a good friend—my director of photography then and to this very day—turned to me and said, "We know what we shot." That's a phrase I repeat to myself all the time when I feel like the editing is not coming along the way I planned. If you know that you filmed *what* you wanted, the *way* you wanted it, be patient and know that the first cut is the deepest (meaning the choppiest). Don't panic!

> **TIP** *If you also do production, the more experience you gain as an editor, the more confident you will be about the elements you need to film. That's called shooting to edit. When you shoot to edit, sometimes it just takes a few attempts at editing to get things to come out the way you planned.*

My music supervisor told me not to worry—the film just needed music. But he knew even less about movies than I did, considering this was his first rodeo in film production as well. Scott and I knew that we needed to go back to the drawing board. What do two kids, with one film production degree between us and no mentors, do when they need film guidance? Of course, they watch a bunch of movies.

We watched *Any Given Sunday*, *Gladiator*, *Pulp Fiction*, and *Stomp the Yard*. (Scott's idea on that last one.) After the movie marathon, we compared notes and realized two things:

- We had very different tastes and observations about movies, which we deemed a good thing in this situation.

- We noticed that movies hardly ever fade to black after a scene, and when they did it represented the passage of time.

We went back and watched our film again, noting that each scene faded to black at the end and faded up from black to start. Now we knew that was a problem. How big of a problem? We were about to find out.

We went back to the library the next day and got rid of every single fade to black between scenes. What did we replace them with? Nothing. We just hard cut from scene to scene. Sixteen hours later, we had a new DVD to watch. The film was still awful, but for different reasons. By just switching the fade to blacks with hard cuts, we transformed a story that was too slow and boring into one that was too fast and hard to comprehend. And now the emotion was gone—removed from the film completely.

When we were done watching that version of the film, Scott and I looked at each other and knew we were thinking the same thing: "Wow. Look how much we changed the film without changing anything."

This is where film editing is so fascinating. We didn't change a single cut. All we did was change the way scenes were edited together—and yet we changed the whole movie. We knew we had gone too far with changing all the fade to blacks with hard cuts, and we realized we needed to land somewhere in the middle. That's when we discovered the meaning of rhythm and how powerful it is.

We realized that fading to black between each scene was giving the film too many moments of closure. When we compared our film with films that were similar in length and style, we observed how seldom the filmmakers faded to black between scenes. They only did it in moments when they purposely wanted the viewers to sit back and think about the events they just watched. And we also realized that providing so much closure was giving the viewers too much time to think. When viewers think too much, they may remind themselves that it's just a movie. That's not a good thing. Of course, the viewers are aware they're watching a movie, but your job as filmmaker and editor is to make them forget that—even if it's just for a minute. This has more to do with rhythm than anything. If a film has a constant rhythm or *beat* to it, the viewers must stay engaged. Think about it on a micro level. Think about one of your favorite TV sitcoms. I think *The Big Bang Theory* is great for this example, but you can use *Friends, Seinfeld,* or anything in that realm. Its rhythm has a beat to it. It goes, line, line, joke, line, line, joke. That's what I'm talking about with scene-to-scene flow.

After careful study of other films and trial and error, we determined that we had too many fade to blacks between scenes. And we realized that replacing them all with hard cuts was not the solution. When we configured the film to have a good blend of fades and hard cuts between scenes, the film improved.

The moral of that story is not about how we transitioned from scene to scene, because it never really was perfect. The point is that something so simple can have such a major effect on the film and even the story.

Then we asked ourselves whether we could apply the rhythm concept inside a single scene. But how could we if there was no opportunity for fading to black? This is where separation of the story comes into play. It took years of practice, trial and error, and mimicking great filmmakers to realize that rhythm is a separate idea from pacing. Rhythm is something you need to keep track of through the entire story.

Let's explore the four elements of rhythm—viewer digestion, transitions, time, and separation—and then tie them together with a bird's-eye view of everything you've learned to this point.

Viewer Digestion:
The Viewer's Need to Process

The first element of rhythm is *viewer digestion* or *viewer processing*. This element is why you care about rhythm in the first place. Let's go all the way back to the plot arc, as most lessons originate and are applied there. Remember that the exposition (beginning) of a story should get viewers thinking, asking questions about the story, and coming up with predictions about what's going to happen. How in the world can they do that if your film doesn't shut up for a second and let them think?

> **OUT OF ORDER MOVIE** *A great example of audience digestion occurs at timecode 1:19:13 in* Out of Order (**FIGURE 5.1**) *Watch the whole interview, the tail end of this scene, and the transition into the scene that follows. When the interview scene ends, notice how much time lapses before another word is spoken. Why? Because I allowed time for the viewers to digest the events that just occurred.*

FIGURE 5.1 Pauses in dialogue and between scenes, such as during this interview scene in *Out of Order*, allow viewers to process what just happened.

Thinking Like a Stand-Up Comedian

I want you to stop reading right now and look up any stand-up comedian on YouTube. If you want a recommendation, I suggest Louis CK or Dave Chappelle.

I'll wait right here.

What you'll notice about these guys, besides their uncanny timing and comedic genius, is they give you time to laugh at their jokes. When a comedian performing live tells a joke and the audience members burst out in laughter, the comedian waits to continue. Whether it's a two-second laugh or a ten-second round of applause, comedians don't continue with their next joke until the laugher starts to fade. Why? Because you're paying them to make you laugh, that's why. And if they start ruining your laughs, why did you go in the first place? Stand-up comedy is the best example of *audience digestion* for that reason. Stand-up comedians will not talk over your laughter, because if they do, you won't laugh again—for fear of missing something, and because it would be rude. The viewers need time to process.

The stand-up comedian has a live audience to play off of, but the editor doesn't.

Film editing works the same way, with one major difference: The stand-up comedian has a live audience to play off of, but the editor doesn't. The editor needs to anticipate how the majority of the audience will react to any given moment. That's what makes it very difficult.

You need to think about viewer digestion within a scene and throughout the overall story in the same way a stand-up comic does. If a moment in a scene is meant to be funny, then you, the editor, need to give the viewers time to chuckle. But it's not just about the funny parts of your film. Your job is to give viewers time to digest and process all their emotions, right in the middle of the scene, without making them feel as if the film is dragging on. It's called *rhythm* because the story stops briefly while the audience digests, and then it keeps going.

Stopping the Story While the Film Rolls On

In the pilot of *Breaking Bad*, Walter White goes to the doctor. He's sitting in the doctor's office, and the doctor tells him he has cancer. Very shortly into the doctor's speech, his audio fades out, and we hear this ear-ringing sound effect. Then we start seeing shots of the doctor's face, and then a close-up of his shirt collar. At this point, we haven't actually heard the word *cancer*. But the editor gives us time to think about what the doctor might be saying. That lasts for about five seconds—a lifetime in film editing—before we're told for certain. Those five seconds were all about audience digestion, processing, and speculation. These moments happen in film all the time.

In the film *The Aviator*, after Hughes has his freak-out scene, Ava Gardner is shaving his face for him. After she turns on the water, an extreme close-up of the stream of water lasts for about three seconds. This is followed by a three-second shot of Hughes looking at the stream of water. This gives the viewers time to feel exactly what Howard feels—which is the OCD taking over his mind.

In the film *Moneyball*, Billy Beane hires Peter Brand to be his assistant GM. The first day on the job, Brand hands Beane a stack of paper and says, "Here are the player breakdowns you asked me to do." Beane says, "I asked you to do three. How many did you do?" Then he flips through papers that clearly number more than three. Brand responds, "Forty-seven." Then, a few seconds later, he says, "Fifty-one. I don't know why I lied just then." The first few times I saw this I laughed at that moment, and I didn't miss anything because Brad Pitt looked at Jonah Hill with a smirk similar to the one I had on my face. The point is: I was given a brief moment to not only chuckle, but realize the chemistry between the two characters.

What do those three examples have in common?

During the moment provided for audience digestion, no new story information was given to the viewers. It can't be audience digestion if the viewers are still receiving new information about the story. That's why I say the story stops while the film keeps on going—and the audience has no idea. And that's why audience digestion is a key element to rhythm, right in the middle of a scene.

Now, how do you execute audience digestion? With separation.

Separation: Techniques for Giving Viewers Some Time

Separation is the *way* you allow the viewers to digest, process, question, debate, or engage in any other form of participation in your story. Creating separation between scenes is fairly easy, so I'll begin there. Creating separation right in the middle of a scene, however, is fairly difficult.

First, let me say that it's not so much about *how* you create separation as it is about knowing *when* you need to create separation. As everything usually does, it comes back to the arc. Like pacing, there are no real rules for when to create separation, but you can use the story arc as a guide. There will be times—as you become a more experienced editor and as you develop a style—that you'll find the need to create separation in less-obvious places than following the arc.

Separation Between Parts of the Story Arc

Let me offer a good guideline for where to start. As I'm sure you recall, the story arc is broken into five basic parts: exposition, rising action, climax, falling action, and resolution. Between each part of the arc, you should be thinking about creating separation. It's during the transition between those parts of the arc that the audience should have time to digest. I'll give you some examples to help you understand why the audience may need time to process what you're telling them. After exploring the concept of when to create separation, we'll look at the many ways to create separation.

The most basic and raw example is a fade to black at the end of a dramatic scene. The screen stays black for two to four seconds, and then the film starts again. The viewers know the film isn't over because the story is clearly unresolved. As you recall from my story at the beginning of this chapter, fading to black after every scene kills your rhythm. However, strategically placing a fade to black in the spots where you need it is perfect for separation. Maybe once or twice per film would you be able to transition between scenes like that and achieve separation.

Fading to black isn't the only way to do that, by the way. You could replace the fade to black with a series of static, exterior shots. It's the exact same concept with the exact same goal. As long as you don't feed the viewer any new information or emotion about the story, they will focus on what you recently provided. This separation allows for audience digestion. I'll give you more creative ways to do this later on—for now, the important thing is being able to identify when you actually need to do this. You can't do it too often, but you need to do it sometimes. The only thing worse than a film that has too much separation is a film that goes 150 miles per hour without stopping. In that case, the viewers have no time to feel anything.

Consider the film *The Social Network*, which won the Oscar for Best Film Editing. The film is all dialogue with many talking heads, which is difficult for an editor to make interesting. There is an unforgettable moment in the film when Sean Parker and Mark Zuckerberg are sitting in a nightclub. Parker is telling Zuckerberg the story of how Victoria's Secret got its start. It's a very powerful story, and it marks the beginning of the film's climax. Parker is using the story as an analogy to make Zuckerberg understand how big his idea for Facebook really is. Then Parker says, "As a show of good faith while you're getting into 100 schools, I'll put you on two continents." This occurs after Parker asks Zuckerberg what his plan is for the summer to grow Facebook.

Then Zuckerberg invites Parker to come live with him and his buddies in their house. This is the obvious turning point in the story because Parker and Eduardo, Zuckerberg's friend and partner, hate each other. This scene reveals the beginning of Eduardo's eventual fate in being kicked out of the company. At the conclusion of this scene a *montage* begins, showing the Winklevoss twins, who claim Zuckerberg stole Facebook from them. These guys are represented as the rich jocks at Harvard who row crew and Zuckerberg is represented as the awkward outcast. The new scene goes on for a solid minute and a half, which is a long time for separation. The twins actually racing has no bearing on the story whatsoever. None, zero, nada. It's there to give you time to think about what just happened and speculate on what might happen. That's it.

> **TIP** *A montage is a series of clips that suggest the passage of time.*

Sometimes we need five seconds of separation and sometimes we need a minute. The ending of the Winklevoss sequence shows them losing the race, which is symbolic of their losing the race in making Facebook. However, that is not new information that's important to the film. That's how you bring symmetry into this equation (see Chapter 4 for more on symmetry). Also, when you watch the film, you'll notice the symmetry (the symbolism of them losing the race) happens right when the separation gives the viewer time to process. Their losing the race doesn't move the story from point A to point B. The next scene *is* important, and the race is important to establish where they are. But showing the race for that long was clearly done to let the audience stew in what they just saw and think about what will happen. And its placement is right, because the climax is starting—it's separation allowing audience digestion during a transition between parts of the plot arc. That kind of thing happens in every movie at various times. The audience doesn't see it or realize it, but moments of separation are there so the audience can play catch-up.

You can achieve separation between parts of the story in other ways, and using B-roll is an important one. The way you use B-roll to create separation determines whether your separation is successful (see Chapter 2 for more on B-roll). The most common way films use B-roll is through exterior city shots, which may or may not feature a character.

> **TIP** Be creative. Try to invent new ways to create separation. The more you execute this philosophy, the more you'll be thinking about it before you edit. Most filmmakers are involved in all areas of production, so planning your moments of separation in advance will help you branch out into more creative ideas and ways to accomplish it.

Creating separation between each part of the arc is a good guideline, but it's by no stretch of the imagination the rule. Chapter 1 mentions that the falling action can sometimes be grouped with the climax to create an extended climax. A large part of fusing the climax and the falling action together comes down to your choice on whether to create separation between the two plot points.

Separation at the Scene Level

When taking the concept of separation deeper, into the scene level of the story, you must still remember the arc. At the scene level, creating separation between plot points becomes even more of a guide than on the larger scale. Remember, each scene is its own arc, which means it has all the characteristics of the overall arc; separation is not excluded from this. You've seen separation in many scenes without even realizing it. Not every scene does it, but most do.

Creating separation in the middle of a scene is different than creating separation in the overall arc. If you fade to black in the middle of a scene, it's not going to work. In scenes, you rely on the acting or action of the character. You should almost be taking your cues from the actors. On the level of a single scene, achieving separation can be as simple as a character stopping to think.

Think about the famous "red pill or blue pill" scene from *The Matrix*. The scene is five minutes long with a very clear breakdown.

The exposition is when Neo walks in; Morpheus greets Neo and says it's an honor to meet him. They sit down and Morpheus starts his dialogue, giving us—and Neo—the information we need to continue with the story, as all expositions do. They talk about the concept of fate.

Then comes the rising action, where Morpheus explains what the Matrix is and how Neo can see that. Then Morpheus presents the two pills and explains what each pill means. Then he offers him a choice: the red pill or the blue pill.

Neo stops and think about that choice. His internal debate lasts for six seconds. That's quite long for separation, but it's justified, considering the magnitude of the decision. An average pause in a scene lasts two to three seconds. Neo's moment of thought *is* the separation. Now, you're probably thinking that this is just what Keanu Reeves did, and the way the scene was directed. It was most likely written like that. Taking time to think about his choice is what Neo would really do. Well, *exactly*. Separation is supposed to mimic the moments of thinking, processing, and anything else that you can dramatize with a pause. The audience is Neo here. This is a first-person narrative, and you want the viewers to think like Neo. (Of course, he takes the red pill. But until it happens, the viewers can speculate.)

> The proper length of separation should become second nature for you as an editor.

Take your cues from the actors or subjects and you will never go wrong. But remember, you control the length of the separation. Maybe Neo paused for 15 seconds, maybe he paused for three, but in the final film it's six seconds—which the editor controlled. The proper length of separation should become second nature for you as an editor. It's similar in all types of films. For example, in a documentary, maybe you have an interview in which a person speaks very slowly. You can control the speaking speed by trimming their pauses.

> **TIP** As the editor, separation is something you control. Most likely, you will modify it compared to the raw clip. To develop this instinct, practice and observe how it's done in other films. Pick a film you've seen before, and watch it just to observe its scene separation.

Transitions:
Getting from Here to There

I want to say up-front that the information in this section is strictly my opinion on this matter. By no means am I presenting this information as fact. However, I suggest that you take my advice: Transitions are not a good thing to lean on or use a lot. In any editing program, you'll find a folder with dozens of premade transitions, ready for you to use. Resist the temptation to use them all.

I only use three transitions—ever:

A fade to black isn't exactly a transition because you aren't transitioning to another clip. But we consider it a transition anyway. Films often fade up from black at the beginning or fade to black at the end. You can also use a fade to black somewhere in the film to create separation. Fading to black in the middle of a film is intended to represent the passage of time. The longer the screen is black, the more time the viewers will assume passes. That means the fade to black actually advances the story. There's a variation called a dip to black. It's exactly the same thing except you're fading to black between two clips, and it happens much quicker. The dip to black is almost too quick to represent time passing; instead, the viewer usually perceives it as representing a move to a different location. It's not used much in films, but it's very common in commercials and movie trailers.

A crossfade is the most common transition—and the most abused. A *crossfade* is when two clips blend over each other; the old clip fades out while the new clip fades in. The standard justification is that it looks cool. So what?! By now you should know better than to do anything just because it looks cool. You need to have a reason that advances the story. Using a crossfade to show the passage of time is the most common correct usage. You can also use it to transition to another scene between two wide exterior shots. I wouldn't do that, but there's a time and a place for everything. A stylistic choice for using a crossfade would be to connect two characters in different locations. You see this often: A good example of this is in the film *Wedding Crashers*. The film uses a crossfade to illustrate that two characters are thinking about each other and falling in love. It's a long crossfade between two faces, and you assume they are feeling the same thing. That's not so much a crossfade as it is an *overlay,* but it's still basically two images blended together. A crossfade starts with one image, and the second image fades in on top of it and eventually takes over the screen completely.

The overlay is two images on top of each other, just like the crossfade, except neither one takes over the screen. They just stay on the screen together until you decide to end the overlay or end the scene.

A dip to white represents traveling backward in time. It works the same way as a dip to black except the screen goes white instead of black. You are likely to use it the least of all options.

> **TIP** Transitions can become a tempting crutch, especially when an editor is struggling with timing cuts. Master the cut and don't lean on transitions. Cut is king, cut is king, cut is king. That's my main lesson when it comes to transitions. Every time you're about to use a transition, ask yourself whether you'd pay for it. If the transition is worth money in the budget to you, then maybe you can think about going for it. Bottom line: You'll often find a well-timed cut is the best solution to any transition.

Time: Managing the Illusion

One of the first rules of pacing is that it has nothing to do with time. Pacing, once again, is just where you decide to cut between clips.

Rhythm is just the opposite. Rhythm really is the mastering of time. Time in film is a fascinating concept, and there are very few rules about it. After touring the country three times teaching film editing, the most common question I've been asked is, "How long should my film be?" That's a very vague question with no real answer. Are you making a feature-length narrative film that can run 50 minutes and beyond? Are you making a television episode that will fall in the 47-minute mark for an hour time slot with commercials? Are you making a short film that can be anything under 50 minutes? Are you making a commercial—web commercial, TV commercial, YouTube ad, 30 seconds, 60 seconds? Are you making a wedding film or an event film? Here's my answer: "Your film should be as long as it is good."

If you follow that rule, you will like the results. Length is only an illusion, because the entire concept of time is an illusion. If you have an hour-long documentary, and you love the first 30 minutes and the last 10 minutes, but you believe there's a weak 20-minute middle section, start cutting. Do not get married to any one section or scene in any film you ever make. It's easier said than done. I know firsthand how painful it can be to cut something you love. Chances are, if that part of the story is dragging, it's because you're not gaining any new information about the story.

But when it comes to length, there is no rule other than the one I just proposed. If you follow the guidance in this book, you won't often worry about running time.

In some cases, running time is dictated for you. Music videos and commercial spots have predetermined running times. Since you know in advance what the running time is to a music video, chances are you'll be able to avoid making a video that is *too long*. Music videos average three minutes, whereas commercials average 30 seconds. In those situations, length isn't really an issue. The issue with length is being able to sustain viewer interest over an extended period of time. Your biggest problem with music videos and commercials is feeling as if you don't have *enough* time. That's a great problem to have. I'd rather leave the viewer wanting more than begging for it to be over.

> As the editor, you must completely control the illusion of time.

The study of time in film doesn't have much to do with the length of a film. Rather, it centers on managing the illusion of time in the story. How do you speed up time? How do you slow it down? How do you show time passing and make it clear to the viewer? As the editor, you must have a firm understanding about how to completely control the illusion of time. That's what this section is about.

Montages: Condensing Time

Simply put, a montage is a collection of short shots edited together to condense space, time, and information. It's a common technique in all forms of filmmaking. As complex as a montage may seem to the eye, it's the most basic way to control and manipulate time in a film. A montage is an easy way to tell viewers that they're experiencing something in a story in a condensed timeframe.

Great examples are found in the *Rocky* films. The scenes where Rocky is training for his next fight usually happen in three minutes or less. The montages use that now-famous soundtrack and incorporate many different scenes. Viewers know Rocky didn't train for a fight in three minutes, three hours, or even three days. These training montages cover *months*. We know that as viewers. Why?

As viewers, we already know that time is not real in films. This is something that's universally known and accepted. A film is *built* by condensing time. When we see ten clips of Rocky—in different locations, hitting punching bags, doing sit-ups, and sparring with Apollo Creed—we know a lot of time has passed. How much exactly? Who cares? Days, weeks, months, years. Sometimes as little as an hour or minute can be summed up in a montage. The exact amount of time doesn't matter. The viewers quickly get the point from a montage.

Without the use of montages, it would be extremely difficult to adapt books to movies. You can thank Sergei Eisenstein, the father of the montage. He was a Soviet film director and film theorist who believed that the montage was essential to cinema. He was right.

When a famous book is adapted to a film, you often hear an uproar from fans complaining about how things were changed or left out. Books are long, very detailed, and told with printed words rather than pictures and audio dialogue. Films are comparatively short, but they can say things with visuals that books cannot. And TV shows can say the same things without being so short. For example, *Game of Thrones* is an amazing adaptation from book to screen. A movie adaptation may run about two hours per book. *Game of Thrones* runs about ten hours per book. Yet it still has to condense time on a very grand scale.

If you're a fan of the show but never read the books, they're long. Every chapter is told from the perspective of one character, and that perspective changes in every chapter. One of the most famous episodes is "Blackwater," the ninth episode of season 2. Watching the Battle of Blackwater Bay on the show took about 20 minutes. Reading that battle scene in the book took me hours, even days, to get through. The book has to paint a picture with words, which takes a lot of time. But the show doesn't need three paragraphs to describe how many men came storming the beach. The show can communicate that in five seconds, with much more impact. This is where the montage comes into play. We as viewers know the battle didn't last 20 minutes. It lasted hours upon hours.

This comes back to using built-in audience information. The filmmakers know the viewers will automatically assume that more time has passed than they're shown. In this situation, book-to-screen adaptations take a lot of unjustified heat. The Blackwater episode needed to happen as the ninth episode of the season because that's where *Game of Thrones* has its big episodes. If they had just adapted the book exactly how it was written, the battle wouldn't have happened then. Filmmakers need to speed up time (or sometimes slow down time) in order to make certain events happen at certain points. Sometimes this calls for the reordering of events or even changing a few events.

It's even worse for movies. A movie such as *The Hunger Games* has less than two hours to tell the story the book told. That's why Katniss doesn't train for 40 minutes of the film. We get it. Show us a few little quick scenes that represent chapters upon chapters of training and move on. Montages are extremely efficient in that way—that's why montages are essential to the filmmaking process.

I want to explore two types of montage. They look the same, they are edited the same way, they can even be similar in length. The only difference is their purpose.

- The self-contained montage
- The transitional montage

SELF-CONTAINED MONTAGE

The *self-contained* montage is a montage within one scene. It's fairly simple. It works the same way any montage does—condensing space, time, and information inside one specific scene. *Space* refers to how much of the film you're taking up. If I condense a task that takes five minutes on screen into 30 seconds, I'm saving space but not losing information. *Time* refers to time in the film. If I pass time quicker, I'm condensing time.

Think about a scene of someone baking muffins, cupcakes, brownies, and other baked goods for a bake sale. The montage would consist of the character baking these things in a kitchen. You wouldn't need to show the character getting the ingredients at the store or selling items at the bake sale. This montage is confined to baking.

> **NOTE** *A self-contained montage usually takes place over minutes or, at most, hours. It almost never covers more than a day.*

Say you have a scene with a wife taking her husband along on a shopping trip for a new dress. Every man reading this knows such a journey could take hours, which could feel like days. Every woman reading this knows it doesn't happen as often as it should, and when it does, it's over way too soon. As the editor, always keep your eye on the emotions of different target audiences. You want to connect with both the men and women in the audience. Don't favor men because you're a man. Ladies, don't make us look like we hate shopping; we really don't have anything better to do.

This scene would be a good time for a self-contained montage. You could do this two ways. You could keep the montage inside one store, or you could spread it out over the entire mall.

Keeping the scene in one store gives you a self-contained montage. If the woman tries on ten dresses, that might take an hour or two in real time—at least in my experience, anyway. As the editor, you *do* want the male viewers to relate, and you want to bring them just to the point that they are getting bored. Yes, that's right. You want the men to be *almost* bored—a realistic translation of what it would be like if they were there. Remember, the viewers will always compare what they see to their own experiences in one way or another.

You want the women to enjoy the montage and feel like it's over way too fast. This montage shouldn't be any more than a minute, depending on the total length of the film. Self-contained montages usually don't last longer than a minute. They can, but the situation would really need to call for it. It should contain shots of the woman finding clothes on the rack, entering the dressing room, and looking at each outfit she chooses (maybe in a jump-cutting sequence as discussed in Chapter 4). The montage should also contain shots of the bored man, possibly giving a yay or nay response to each outfit. Here's the cool thing: The order of shots doesn't matter. You can show shots of her gathering clothes off the rack, then checking herself out in the outfits, and then jump back to the beginning when she's getting clothes off the racks again. You can even be fancy and edit a little mini story for each outfit. For example, woman takes outfit off the rack, women tries on outfit, man gives his approval (or not). Then repeat. The random order doesn't matter because the information in the montage is gathered overall in the viewers' mind, not as it's seen sequentially.

> *Self-contained montages usually don't last longer than a minute.*

The moment your two characters step outside that store and start shopping for other things at other places, it's no longer a self-contained montage. Now you have a transitional montage.

TRANSITIONAL MONTAGE

A transitional montage takes place over many scenes and represents a longer time period—maybe a day or even years. It is the one thing in editing that uses constant repetition to tell the story: The more times you see a particular action in a different setting, the more time you will assume has passed. This is not the same as showing something once and then repeating it in some way later in the story. Transitional montage uses constant, one-after-the-other repetition.

Usually, the transitional montage is used to *transition* into another part of the story, often at the end of the first or second act. The transitional montage uses several scenes to illustrate that a lot of time is passing—like the *Rocky* montages. The *Rocky* montages show him training over the course of months, doing several different things in several different places. He's not just training in one room, doing one exercise. By showing him sparring, running, hitting the speed bag, and doing various other training activities, the audience perceives it to be *months* of training as opposed to a long day of training. That is the difference between a self-contained montage and a transitional montage.

Slowing Down Time

When it comes to controlling time, using a montage is not the only option. In addition, it's not always about speeding up time for efficient storytelling. Sometimes, you want to slow down time—maybe even slower than real time.

10, 9, 8, 7, 6, 5, 4—think of a scene in a movie when someone is defusing a bomb, and they have ten seconds to do it. Next time that happens, pull out your stopwatch—or, if you live in the 21st century, your smartphone—and time the countdown in real time. You'll notice it's the longest ten seconds in the history of time.

> **TIP** *Time isn't real in film.*

If you use montages to speed up time and provide a lot of information, you actually have the time to slow things down when you want. This also produces a major contrast, so the viewers really feel when time is moving slower. What's the difference, and how will you know when to speed up or slow down time?

In a word, the decision comes down to *intensity*.

As an editor, when you encounter a moment of intensity in film, you want to live in that moment as long as you possibly can. On the other hand, when you're simply trying to relate information to the viewers, you want to get through that moment as quickly as you can.

The general rule is, if the moment is intense, you want to be in real time or slower. You need to come to terms with intensity—your highs and lows. Not every moment is intense. Look at moments around the rising action, climax, and falling action. I'm not saying intense moments don't happen in the exposition or resolution, but they're less likely to be there.

Watch the film *Any Given Sunday* to analyze its conflict and time control. The film consists of many montages and moments that move slower than real time, and it's a very good example of the contrast between the two. Like any sports movie, it's littered with montages, including one with several football games crammed into a single transitional montage in the middle of the film. When they get to the last game the viewers see, that's when real time slows down. On the final play of the film, there are four seconds left on the clock. Al Pacino's character says, "Four seconds is a lifetime. We're a lifetime away here." His team needs to score a touchdown to win, and they have four seconds to do it. Then the ball is hiked. This "four-second play" lasts a little longer than a minute.

How is that presented without feeling as if it's dragging on and on? Well, there are a million ways to do that, but this film uses flashbacks and dozens of cutaways to players, fans, commentators, TV screens, extreme close-ups of the main character's eyes, and much more. It also uses *slow motion*.

> **TIP** Remember, if you never speed up time in a film, then slowing it down doesn't have the same effect. For viewers to feel the impact of slower time, you need to provide a visual comparison.

▶ SLOWING DOWN WITH SLOW MOTION

One way you can cheat time is by stretching it out using slow motion. When you use slow motion in film, it takes the viewers out of the concept of time altogether. You don't *have* to use slow motion to slow down time, by any means, but it has the advantage of making viewers immediately forget all about time. It's definitely cheating. But if you're not cheating, you're not trying.

Speeding Up Time

Editors have many options for speeding up time that don't involve the use of montages. This brings me to my seven rules for speeding up time.

> **TIP** *The passing of time in a story should be your last concern. Pacing and rhythm rule over time—always.*

1. TIME PASSING BETWEEN SCENES IS IMPLIED

The time that passes between scenes will be inferred by viewers. Don't feel the need to constantly establish exactly how much time has passed, or what the actual time is in your story. Unless the specific time is part of the story, it's not relevant.

In many films, people are given a deadline to do something—*or else.* In that situation, time does matter. However, most of the time people will assume how much time has passed, and they'll be surprisingly right. Let's say you have a scene of a guy talking to a girl on the phone, and he says, "OK, I'll meet you for dinner tonight at that place on Fourth Street." You could cut to the next scene and show this man and women, mid-conversation, eating dinner, and the passage of time would be assumed. It's *later.* They're at the dinner they just talked about. Who cares what the time is? Viewers understand the natural progression of time.

You could also use that same conversation followed by a long fade to black at the end of the phone call. Then, cut into the next scene when the couple is clearly deep into a relationship. Maybe they're at a park, where he proposes to her. For this to be a believable outcome, you would need to share key information before the phone call. But as far as time passing between scenes, viewers will assume that the characters have developed a healthy relationship over time.

> **TIP** *When editing, don't be concerned about how much time is passing between scenes, and don't worry that the viewers won't understand. They will. Films don't follow the rules of time in the reality sense. Films are given the freedom to play with time, traveling through it at the speed the filmmakers see fit. It's only when you are jumping back and forth in time that you need to be concerned with telling the viewers where they are in "time."*

Keep in mind that the first example used a hard cut between the phone call and the dinner that happens later that night. The second example used a long fade to black between the phone call and the much later proposal scene. That simple fade to black represents a long passage of time.

> **OUT OF ORDER MOVIE** *At timecode 1:15:00 in* Out of Order, *notice that when the scene ends and the next scene starts, it's easy to understand that some time has passed (**FIGURE 5.2**). How much time—five minutes or two hours—is not relevant to the story.*

FIGURE 5.2 During this phone call, the main character agrees to meet a man at a coffee shop. When the next scene starts, it's apparent that time has passed—but it doesn't matter how much time.

2. YOU CAN PASS TIME IN THE MIDDLE OF A SCENE WITHOUT LEAVING THE SCENE

This is a difficult thing to do, but always remember that in a film, *time is not real*. Let's say you have a scene with two people eating dinner. You want to show their conversation before they order and then show more conversation toward the end of the meal. The simple solution is to do what most TV shows do: Show an exterior of the building (or even go to a different scene) before returning for the second half of the scene. That's an option for sure. But maybe you don't want the viewers to break their connection with these two characters.

You might try one of these options:

- **Use B-roll to advance the scene.** You can use B-roll from the scene to separate the two parts of the conversation. This is something you can do when you want to cut out the middle of someone's conversation because it slows down the film.

- **Use a self-contained montage.** A self-contained montage of the characters laughing, drinking, and eating—in combination with B-roll—works to separate the two parts of the scene.

OUT OF ORDER MOVIE Watch the Out of Order *movie from timecode 1:36:24 to 1:37:47, which is actually two scenes in one (**FIGURE 5.3**). It's a unique way to show the passage of time because it doesn't cut away from the scene. When you do this, it's important to think outside the box. Note the importance of treating the two parts of the scene as separate scenes.*

FIGURE 5.3 Notice how smoothly time passes in these two scenes.

3. TIME-LAPSE INDICATES HOW TIME PASSES

Time-lapse is the best way to pass time: You show a scene ending at night followed by a time-lapse of it turning to daytime. This has the advantage of showing viewers exactly how much time passed. Just be careful not to get sucked into using this trick way too often because it looks so good. Try limiting yourself to one time-lapse per film.

4. SAVE TIME BY IMPLYING ACTION

Let's say you have a character at a fast-food counter ordering a burger and fries. She pays, and then the worker gets the food. In real time, it takes a minute or two to complete a fast-food order. But film time isn't real time. Show the character waiting long enough to give the viewers a sense of waiting, and then bring in the food. You don't want the food to appear instantly, but making viewers sit through such an everyday occurrence in real time would kill the rhythm of your film.

> **TIP** *Remember, you need to save time to tell your story. Your most-used technique for doing that is likely to be cutting the time characters spend waiting. It's all about implying the action of the character offscreen. If viewers will understand what's happening, especially in a mundane activity, why bother showing it? Cut to the next action and be done with it.*

5. CUT DOWN TRAVEL TIME

If you want to make the world's most boring film, just show a bunch of people walking to their destinations. Believe me, it will work. As an editor, you'll be handed clips of characters walking in real time, from many different angles. Cutting that stuff is a good way to trim the fat of your film. Cut down the walking and waiting significantly. Why not cut it completely? Well, because movement is life. Walking gives the illusion the story is moving forward. You need to show it, but tastefully.

For example, say you have a shot from the front and back of a guy walking down a hallway. You should be able to cut two-thirds of the walking time out of the shot—unless something vital to the story happens during the walk. If the goal is to get the character from point A to point B, you only want to show 30 percent of that walk, maximum. Here's the cool thing about this: The viewers won't even notice.

6. USE TIME TRAVEL (FORWARDS OR BACKWARDS)

Stories often travel backwards, and sometime forwards, in the story timeline. If you use flashbacks or flash-forwards, be creative with the editing as they are difficult for viewers to grasp. I like to use a long white fade to move backwards in time. It's the opposite of the long black fade, so I assume that viewers will perceive it as a flash-back. A TV show such as *Lost,* which jumped around in time constantly, used a long white flash combined with sound effects to illustrate jumps in time. If viewers don't immediately understand that they've traveled back in time in the story, they will usually catch on after seeing your trick once. It's OK. Don't feel the need to spell out everything for them.

7. JUST IGNORE TIME COMPLETELY

Because time is not real in film, the only rule of time, really, is that there are no rules. It sounds crazy, but every technique of controlling time has been done in film. I was watching *Moneyball* the other day and noticed a scene in which Brad Pitt's character walks in his office and presses a button to listen to a message on his machine. The next thing you know, he's sitting in a chair and talking on the phone. It was like he teleported. It was amazing and seamless.

Tying in the Narrative Perspective and Story Arc

Rhythm relates directly to narrative perspective, which is discussed in Chapter 2. In almost all aspects of editing, you can refer to either your narrative perspective or the story arc to find answers to editing questions. Much of what I say in these chapters is only theory. They are theories that I observe to work in successful and universally loved stories, but theories can be challenged. You can choose whether to incorporate or ignore these theories. If you find yourself stumped on a rhythm question in the editing process—such as when and where to create separation—you can often find the answer in the narrative perspective.

When you are editing a first-person narrative, scene, or story, you want to make the viewers experience it from the perspective of *this specific character.* Consider the example of the woman trying on dresses while the man waits. When told from the woman's point of view, I believe a self-contained montage is the most stimulating and entertaining way to show this moment. Now let's consider the same example, but from the man's point of view. Say he's your main character, and it's a first-person narrative from his perspective. In that case, do you want it to be so entertaining? Remember: Always ask yourself, "What's my goal?"

When told from the man's point of view, you want to illustrate that he's bored out of his mind. Because my character is really bored, I want this boredom to transfer itself to the viewers. Be very careful, though, as this is a slippery slope. I don't want the viewers to be bored *with the film*—or even the scene. I want them to feel my character's boredom. That is tricky, and I would most likely solve it by passing up a montage and going with a standard scene. I would probably make the scene pretty short to avoid boring the viewers too much.

> *Remember: Always ask yourself, "What's my goal?"*

Before making a decision, however, zoom out for a second and look at the surrounding scenes. What led to this moment? Where does the story go from here? The answers to those questions will reveal clues as to how long this scene should be and how bored the viewers can become. Maybe in the next scene, the man dumps the girl because she's the most boring human alive. Then he meets the woman of his dreams in scenes that follow. That's valuable information, and it incorporates the story arc.

The key is that any boredom the viewers feel should be for a reason. Viewers should feel the contrast between boredom and excitement. In this case, I might want viewers to feel what it's like in the day of a life with the boring girl as opposed to a day with the girl of their dreams. Yes, *their* dreams. It's a first-person narrative, so when your character falls in love, your viewers need to fall in love also.

The surrounding scenes will provide context clues as to how long the "boring moment" should last as well. If this boring girl is one of many in a long line of failed relationships, the scene could be two shots long. She comes out in the dress, spins around, and asks, "How do I look?" Cut to a shot of the man with his head in his hands, suffering. It could be that simple. If the scene is the lead-in to something major, then the viewers need to experience it longer, closer to real time. Let the viewers be your character for a little longer. The scene should end right as the viewers have had enough. How do you know when they've had enough? It's the same idea as knowing when they'll laugh at a joke and for how long. Practice practice practice.

As you can see in this example, it's extremely important to be able to identify the story arc and narrative perspective. They can change the entire editing construction for a scene.

▶ EDITING CHECKLIST

Use this checklist to remember all the variables that go into the visual editing of a scene.

1. What part of the story arc am I in?

2. What perspective is this told from?

3. What's the proper pacing of this scene, when does it change, and what causes it to change?

4. Where do the separation points need to be for this scene to create proper rhythm?

5. What's the conflict?

If you're disciplined about asking yourself these five questions every time you edit, you'll teach your brain to always think this way. The more you do it, the faster you'll spot the answers. Once you've mastered this concept, you can then modify it to your own style.

The good news is that the visual part of the story is made of those five questions, and answering them will make you a better editor.

The bad news is that all this is only half the equation. The other half you cannot see—you can only hear.

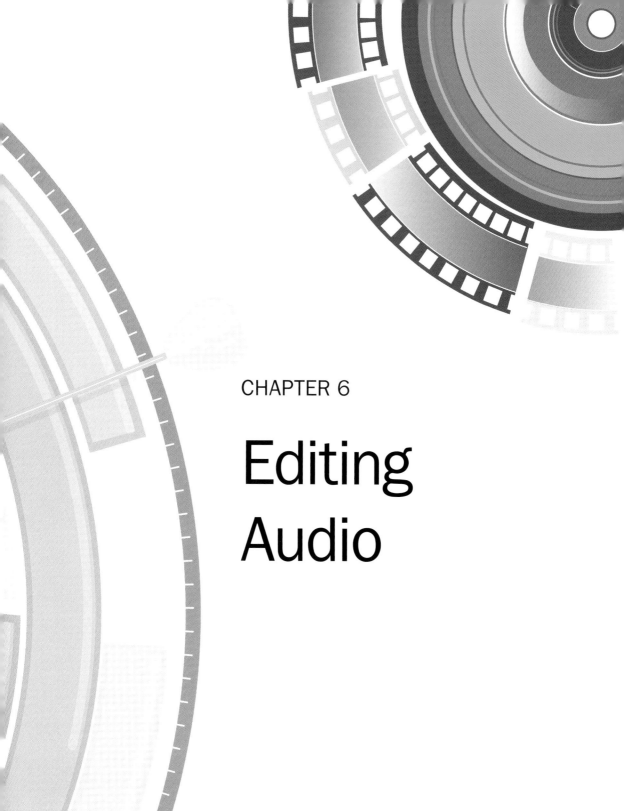

CHAPTER 6

Editing
Audio

Welcome to the enigma of filmmaking. Audio! Yes, that's right, it's a real pain because guess what? None of us are audio engineers and most likely never will be. That's OK. It all comes back to that modern-day filmmaker who wears many hats on set and in postproduction.

Maybe you have dabbled in audio editing or plan to. I'll say up front that I'm not an audio engineer. I know what I'm doing and I understand what to do, but I've sat with enough real, trained engineers to respect the title of *audio engineer*. It's a very difficult trade to learn—and if you want to learn it, by all means, go for it. Audio editing is its own lifetime study, just as video and film editing are lifetime studies.

> *Audio editing is its own lifetime study, just as video and film editing are lifetime studies.*

This chapter explores the other half of film—the sound. I am not covering how to make it sound good, though. Instead, I aim to help you modify sound to better tell your story. Audio is a very powerful thing. When you make a mistake on audio, the audience is much more likely to notice it compared to a visual mistake.

The key to modern-day audio engineering, which I like to call *audio survival*, is understanding the principle of leveling. *Leveling* means making each category of audio the same level of loudness, measured in decibels. All the dialogue should be the same level, all the music should be the same level, and so on.

If you're making a big-budget feature film that will be released in movie theaters, you *need* an engineer and, most likely, can afford one. If you're making your own films, shorts, event videos, commercials, or anything on the south side of millions in the budget, look to the information in this chapter as your audio savior. I should know: I have years of experience messing it all up and watching engineers fix it.

Learning About Audio

I happen to live down the street from the engineer who mixed the song "I Believe I Can Fly" by R. Kelly, which I believe to be part of one of the best-mixed albums of all time. One day I brought him the audio files to a film I was working on and asked him for helping in mixing it. His advice opened my eyes to the crazy and complicated world that is audio. Here's what he had to say:

1. "You can't actually mix anything without all the sounds separated onto separate tracks." This means the music needs to be broken down into all its sounds and parts. That blew my mind. I needed to hand him one track for each instrument—a file for just the drums, just the vocals, just the piano, and so on. Then he would put all the sounds back together, mixed.

2. "I can mix this for you as far as I can go, but movie mixing is different from music. There's an abstract quality to it that I don't understand. Things aren't always supposed to be scientifically correct." That made me feel a lot better because I understand the abstract, he understands the technical, and together we could tackle the challenge together.

Audio does have a lot of science to it, and some of that science is discussed in this chapter. But make no mistake, theories also apply to audio, including theories about pacing. As mentioned in Chapter 4, the goal isn't to teach you how to create perfect pacing, but to teach you the difference between right and wrong pacing. After all, editing really comes down to watching something and knowing that it needs refinements. Audio is similar in that you won't become an engineer overnight, but you can learn the difference between right and wrong. And you can learn many audio tricks that add to the viewing experience.

Now that I've scared the pants off you, let's dig into audio. It's kept me up many nights, so that you may sleep easier. In this chapter, we will look at audio layers, ambient sound, dialogue tracks, sound effects, music, audio being relative to distance, how to use sound to help you make cuts and assemble the film, audio transitions—and a lot more.

Capturing Audio

When it comes to audio, the production matters a great deal. My advice on *recording* audio is: Don't screw up. Easier said than done, I know. But if you mess up the recording, it's often harder to fix than video or film. The key to not messing up your audio recording is to monitor it through headphones and listen to what's around you. If you can see a refrigerator while you're recording, any mic worth its weight in silver will pick that up—loudly. Air conditioners can be the death of audio. Airplanes and cars will kill your audio. You need a quiet environment to record audio, and that may entail unplugging things nearby. If you're at a live event and there's not much you can do, make sure to equip yourself with the right set of mics for the situation.

> **TIP** *For recording in quiet rooms, use a solid shotgun mic (I prefer anything made by Sennheiser). For situations with a lot of background noise, use a lavalier or pin mic (I suggest Rode mics).*

▶ DON'T USE GREAT HEADPHONES

When monitoring audio and editing sound, just use $50 headphones. I use a solid pair of Sony noise-canceling headphones. Your Bose or Beats By Dre will not help you when editing audio. Why? Really good headphones put out what's called *treated sound*. That means the speakers are changing the true sound of what is actually playing. For example, the Beats By Dre headphones pump more bass into the audio than is actually there. I know this because I have them and have done many tests. This is not to say these headphones aren't great for listening to music—they are. But to edit raw audio for a film, you want speakers that are as flat and untreated as possible so you can hear the true sound.

Components of Audio in Film

One difference to understand up-front is that audio is layered while your visuals (video clips) are not. If I stack several audio clips on top of each other on separate tracks (**FIGURE 6.1**), they all play simultaneously. If you stack ten video clips on top of each other on separate tracks, only the top clip displays unless you lower its opacity.

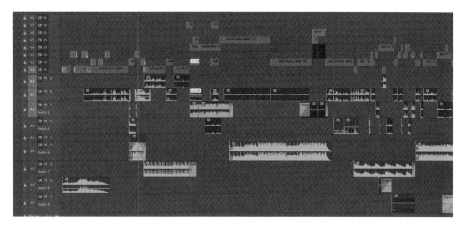

FIGURE 6.1 In film all the audio tracks play at the same time. Mixing audio is the process of making sure each audio track is at its proper level. You have to mix the layers because if they play at the same level, it will sound crowded and too loud.

In filmmaking, audio is broken down into four main components. Among those components, you can have as many different audio sources as you need. For example, one of the four components is a dialogue track. You can choose to have ten, two, or even zero dialogue sources on your dialogue track. Here are the four components of audio:

1. Ambient sound (background sound)

2. Sound effects (added sounds associated with key actions in a film, such as a door knock or a phone ringing)

3. Dialogue (the main track of voices from the characters)

4. Music

Any sound you have in a film will be one of these five components. You might have them all or any combination of the five. Not every film needs all five, by the way. A music video is almost always just music and nothing else. A commercial may be just voiceover, music, and sound effects. The combination you use will not determine the quality of your film. The audio components you use should depend on what you need. However, the more components you have, the more complex the leveling will be. (I talk about levels at the end of this chapter with regard to the audio mix.)

Let's go through these components one by one, but in a slightly different order than they are listed above. Because sound builds on itself, we will start with ambient sound.

> **NOTE** *Voiceover (narration) can also be said to be an audio component, but not a lot needs to be said about it here. You either have it or you don't in your film. Voiceover is handled in mixing.*

Ambient Sound

Editors often forget about ambient sound, but if you do that, you are forgoing one of the most powerful storytelling tricks in your bag. Ambient sound is *atmosphere*. It is any sound in a film that isn't dialogue, music, or sound effects, such as:

- City street noise
- Birds chirping
- The rustle of clothing
- Background voice chatter
- Weather sounds

Each of these examples might also be a sound effect, depending on how it's used. A bird chirping could be a sound effect or ambient sound. The deciding factor is its connection to the story. Yes, even in audio the story matters. If that bird is a part of the story, his chirping is a sound effect. If it is just a part of the environment, it's ambient sound.

> **OUT OF ORDER MOVIE** *Ambient sounds help create the atmosphere you cannot see in scenes. Sometimes it's better to let the viewers imagine than actually showing them everything. At timecode 00:17:49 in the* Out of Order *film, Paul is sitting in a diner with his mother (**FIGURE 6.2**). If you listen closely enough, you can hear background noise such as plates banging, people talking in a low hum, and the occasional bell to indicate food is ready. You are allowed to hear all this because it helps create this atmosphere in your mind. The reality is, the diner is*

closed and a film crew is where the kitchen crew should be. The other reality is, it needs to be very quiet to record the dialogue. However, it comes out too quiet on the real recording, so we added ambient sound to make it feel real. The viewer doesn't notice because that's the way it should sound.

FIGURE 6.2 Ambient sounds, such as background noise in a diner, make scenes feel real.

Room Tone: The Sound of Silence

If you're sitting in quiet room right now, great. If not, you'll have to imagine or remember what it's like. I want you to really listen to the silence in the room you're in. Take it in and listen very closely. Count to ten. Done? Remember that experience and remember it very well, because it's the most basic thing I can teach you about audio: Nothing is ever silent. Even silence makes noise. I'm not talking about the bird chirping or the wind blowing. I'm talking about the actual sound of silence. We call this *room tone*.

Room tone is the most basic form of ambient audio. It is the sound of silence in film—and in life. If you record a voiceover in a professional recording studio, there is no room tone under the voice because recording studios are designed to absorb room tone. But when you record dialogue on set with a shotgun microphone, there will be room tone under the voices. (By the way, this is the difference in sound between dialogue and voiceover. Dialogue has room tone, voiceover doesn't.)

Even when a narrative film goes quiet, you can still hear room tone. If you haven't noticed this, try watching your favorite movie or TV show with headphones at fairly loud volume. You may not think you hear room tone because you've been hearing it in every room you've been in since you were born. Should you worry about room tone? Should you try to get rid of it? No way. In fact, for every shot you ever edit, you need 30 seconds of uninterrupted room tone (I explain why later in this chapter).

> **TIP** Every time you do a shoot, always record 30 seconds of room tone for safety. Just have everyone be quiet, and record a 30-second clip of silence. This room tone recording will help you create consistent sound when you use it in your mix.

Remember, as an editor you're assembling a world that is not real. It's also two-dimensional. Ambient sound helps create the atmosphere—without it, the atmosphere doesn't feel real.

Buy yourself an audio recorder specifically to record room tone. I recommend a Zoom H1 or a Tascam. If you're feeling really cheap, use your smartphone. The quality of recording for ambient audio isn't as important as the quality of the other components. That doesn't mean a bad recording of room tone is OK; it just means that the room tone will be tucked into the background of your final mix. Any flaw in the recording will most likely go unnoticed. At worst case, you can record it with your camera's on-board mic.

Room tone doesn't mean you have to be inside. If you're in the woods, record the sounds of the woods for 30 seconds. If you're on a street corner, record the sound of the street corner. If you're at the beach—and if you are, you're really asking for an audio challenge—record the waves crashing. These sounds help the viewer imagine the setting. Sometimes, letting the viewers imagine the setting is better than showing it to them. The imagination is a great thing. It also forces the viewers to constantly participate in the storytelling process (something I've been harping on since Chapter 1). When the viewers are given a task, it makes the story more participatory. Ambient sound is a great way to do that.

Justifying the Sound: What Was That?

Viewers need a visual reference for what they're hearing in some cases. It starts with known quantities. If a character is walking through an office, past cubicle after cubicle, what should make up the ambient sounds? Phones ringing, papers rustling, people talking, printers printing, fax machines screaming, typing—anything that embodies that setting. If viewers hear these sounds, they'll visualize what is making those sounds. This is how they participate.

Now, what if someone in the office kitchen is pan-frying some peppers? That is an unfamiliar office sound, so your viewers will hear it and say to themselves, "What's that?" In an office setting, the frying sound is not a good thing because it's one of those things that sounds like a mistake. It sounds like a scratchy microphone. To solve that, you need to *justify the sound*. Show the viewers a shot of the peppers frying. After that, they'll link the visual with the sound, and then you can use this sound as part of the ambience. If a sound is unknown or unexpected, you need to show it at some point.

> *OUT OF ORDER MOVIE* *You can see a good example of justifying sound at time-code 21:21 in* Out of Order *(**FIGURE 6.3**). While Paul is talking to the filmmakers, the projector screen comes down. The noise comes out of nowhere. If I never showed a wide shot of the screen coming down, the audience would be con-fused. If you watch this scene from the beginning, you'll notice I use this sound to break the flow of the scene on purpose—to change gears into the rising action of the scene. This is an important moment for the film because it's Brice's first appearance onscreen. I'm basically stopping the story to introduce him. This is a form of separation, as discussed in Chapter 5.*

FIGURE 6.3 The noise of the screen coming down creates visual and audio separa-tion in this scene. The separation helps introduce Brice, who enters, grabs a chair, and sits down.

Removing Ambient Sound for Effect

Providing constant ambient audio in a film—and then suddenly taking it away—is very noticeable. It screams, "Pay attention!" Movies and TV shows do this all the time as a way to draw attention to the most intense moments.

A good example comes from the *Game of Thrones* episode, "Blackwater." A character named The Hound is one of the best fighters in the kingdom. In the middle of a scene with a ton of ambient sounds—people screaming, running, fighting, swords clanging together—it cuts to a first-person perspective of The Hound spotting a man on fire. The ambient audio slowly fades away. Because so much sound just vanishes, the viewers become hyper-focused on the fire. Then The Hound just leaves the battle—which is a big no-no for someone like The Hound. The viewers then know that he is afraid of fire.

The editors subtracted ambient sound to tell a very important part of the story. Viewers did not know this before, and it was never explained until the following season. The subtraction of ambient clued in viewers. If the ambient sound had not been there to remove, half the viewers probably would have missed this point in the story.

Removing ambient sound doesn't always need to serve as a storytelling device. You can use similar strategies to intensify moments. For example, in *The Godfather Part III*, Al Pacino's character is screaming after the death of his daughter. It starts by showing him scream, but all you can hear is music. This effect draws us in and forces us to read into the emotion. Then the editor fades in the sounds of the scream—and back out again. Why? The film is basically fading us in and out of reality.

Sound Effects in Postproduction

A postproduction sound effect, also called a Foley sound effect, is an everyday sound effect added to a film. For example, if I don't like how the recording of footsteps comes out in the film, I may choose to record footsteps after the fact and replace the original footsteps in editing. Postproduction sound effects include any artificial sounds added later, such as glass breaking, bottles opening, gun shots, knocking on doors, and phones ringing.

OUT OF ORDER MOVIE *At timecode 1:02:13 in* Out of Order *you can see light-ning in the background of a dialogue scene (**FIGURE 6.4**). This was a gift and a curse. A gift because I could use the sound effect of thunder to make the scene feel a little more intense. A curse because I had to find a way to not record the real thunder so that I could control where it happened after the fact. I turned the recording volume way down while recording this scene, and then I added the thunder while editing. Throughout the scene, you can hear it in the background, sometimes loud and sometimes a low rumble. Foley sound effects like this allow you to control the strength of the sound in postproduction.*

FIGURE 6.4 As this scene develops, there is an added intensity when lightning appears through a window and thunder rumbles in the background.

Why You Can Exaggerate Sound Effects

When it comes to sound effects, be creative. Sometimes you want to amplify the magnitude of a sound or alter its realism for film. There's not much you can do to reinvent a knock on the door or the ring of a phone. Those sounds are obvious. But how about a punching sound effect? This is the single greatest example of the concept that *movies are movies, not life.*

Pick a movie from the *Bourne* series and watch any of the very well-constructed fight scenes. Sometimes when you're watching a film for enjoyment, it's hard to notice. But if you zero in on the punching sound effects, you'll notice that they sound cartoonish. There is nothing realistic about these sound effects, and yet some of these films were nominated for Best Sound at the Oscars. Why do they work so well then? Because movies aren't reality, as I've mentioned many times.

In the *Bourne* films, the pacing and rhythm are phenomenal. So when a fight scene happens, you're not paying attention to the construction of the scene—you're watching the fight. The speed of light is much faster than the speed of sound. Why does that matter? Because your brain is processing images that arrive at the speed of light while it processes the audio on a slight lag. That lag time doesn't give the brain the opportunity to question the sound, especially when it knows where the sound is coming from. This fact allows sound designers to exaggerate what an effect might sound like. The fight looks real, so the sound is given the benefit of the doubt.

Why not use the actual sound? Well, you'd know if you punch yourself in the face, but please don't. Take my word for it: It doesn't really make a sound. You, the recipient of the hit, make a sound, sure (a grunting noise). If you watch these fight scenes, you'll hear a lot of grunts, which help hide the fake punching sound effects.

When it comes to sound effects, the moral of the story is that if something doesn't make a sound, it doesn't mean there shouldn't be a sound effect for it. Recall the discussion of ambient audio. Taking away the ambient audio is a good technique to intensify a moment, but resorting to silence might not be the best move. Sometimes in those moments, a sound effects can amplify the intensity even more. Think about any film in which a bomb goes off. A lot of times, instead of immediately hearing the aftermath of the explosion we see a character on the ground covering his ears. His ears hurt because they are ringing. And then we hear the sound of ears ringing. In a loud theater, this can actually hurt the viewers' ears as well. If you do this (for just a second), it gives viewers the sense that they were there. It's a great tactic.

You can take away ambient sound at other times, too—for example, in love scenes. You've seen this in movies many times. Boy sees a girl from across the room. All the audio fades out to represent his hyper-focus on the girl. But it's not totally silent. Often, a very low wind sound effect is in the background. Don't ask me why it works, but it works well. I want to say that the wind represents air, and the scene represents the character blocking everything out except the girl and fresh air, but who knows? I imagine that someone tried it a long time ago and people have been doing it ever since. Watch the scene in *Blow* when the characters played by Johnny Depp and Penelope

Cruise meet for the first time. As he sees her, the background chatter gets replaced by a low wind sound effect, and we know he's in love. It's like cheating. And as mentioned in Chapter 5, if you're not cheating, you're not trying.

Dialogue

Of all the audio components, dialogue is the most straightforward, but it's also the hardest to make clean. Eighty percent of dialogue work is done in the field when recording. This means that if you record it clean, the legwork is done. Now you just need to make all the dialogue sound consistent. If you somehow mess up the recording of dialogue, though, the odds of being able to fix it are slim. This is when you go hat in hand to an engineer and hope she can help. And even then, chances are you'll leave with nothing more than a lecture about how important it is to capture a clean recording of your main dialogue track.

Using Room Tone to Help Stitch Together Dialogue

The nature of the dialogue track is that you will most likely have two or more recordings of it. When you record audio for film, depending on your shot selection, different shots pick up the voices in different ways and at different levels. Assume your scene has three characters sitting in a room talking at normal tone and volume.

Wide shot: When you record the wide shot, the mic is positioned above head, out of shot, in the middle of the three characters. It will pick up the voices of the three characters. Of all the recordings, the mic will be the farthest from your characters in the wide shot. You will need to turn up the volume of this recording to have the voice at the same level as the medium and close-up shots. When the volume is turned up, the room tone becomes higher. In addition, the farther the people are from the mic, the more their voices echo.

Medium and close-up shots: Assuming that each of the three characters gets his or her own recorded medium shot, you will get three different-sounding voices. For each character's medium shot, the mic will only record that character. Now, the mic is strong enough to pick up the other characters, but considering it will be positioned above head, just out of the shot of the character you're recording, the off-camera character's audio will most likely be unusable. A medium shot will probably give you the cleanest sounding room tone of all, because as the mic gets closer to the character, the recording volume comes down, which brings the room tone down.

The problem is, after you record all these different clips, when you assemble your scene you need to make the scene sound like one constant stream. The better you record it, the easier it is. However, regardless how well it's recorded, you will always need to do some work to make the audio sound consistent.

Don't panic! First things first. Remember that room tone we talked about? You're about to find out why it's so vital. The wide shot will have the loudest room tone of all the shots. Because it's the loudest, and you can't turn it down without affecting the voices (unless you're an engineer), it needs to be the level of room tone that runs throughout the entire scene. Hopefully, you recorded 30 seconds of room tone before you recorded that wide shot, because you'll be adding it to the other shots.

As I've said before, the best cut is one that viewers fail to notice. Well, if the viewers can hear the room tone changing levels in every cut, they will notice it. And they will probably hate it. All you need to do is mix that louder room tone under the whole scene, and boom: constant room tone throughout the scene. When you cut to a close-up with a clean-sounding voice, viewers still hear the hum of room tone in the background. Yes, ideally you want that room tone as low as possible. But it's better to be consistently bad than inconsistently good.

> *TIP Much of audio mixing is about producing consistent sound. If you have a loud air conditioner that you can't turn off while you're recording, make sure it's consistent throughout the whole scene. Record it like you record room tone. You don't want the audio perfect in some parts and bad in other parts. The audience will quickly forget about the AC noise if it's consistent. That's why refrigerator sounds are so awful. It's bad enough that they're loud, but when they turn off and on in a scene, the sound draws attention and takes the viewers away from the story.*

Room Size and Reverb

Editing dialogue can be much more complex than just adding or subtracting room tone. Sometimes, the location dictates a great deal of what you need to do as the editor. Working with a conversation of three guys sitting in a room is simple. Now put three guys in a tunnel and record that same conversation. If you record the audio the same way, it's going to sound similar as far as the echo (because the closer the guys are to the mic, the less echo there will be). But now the characters are a tunnel, which produces a natural echo. Sure, a tad bit of that will be picked up in the recording, but not enough to make it real. If you want the characters to sound like they are really in a tunnel, it will require postproduction audio work. This is where adding *reverb* comes in. Reverb is a kind of echo that indicates how large a room a sound is happening in.

Here is where your job crosses the line into engineer territory. You can do one of three things in this situation:

1. **Ignore the room and always make the dialogue sound clean (by recording the sound clean and not affecting it in postproduction).**
It's not a bad idea. I do this sometimes because, often, you can do more harm than good when trying to affect the voice if you really don't know what you're doing. If 90 percent of the film has clean and normal sound anyway, the viewers most likely won't care.

2. **Find an audio engineer.** Describe the room type and its dimensions, and the engineer will put a reverb effect on the voice. The engineer will know the exact type of reverb to put on the voice to make it sound realistic to the room the character is in.

3. **Try adding reverb in your editing program.** All editing programs have a reverb sound effect that you can drop onto an audio clip. In fact, most come with preset reverb levels to put you on the right path: Tunnel, Long Hallway, Small Room, Large Room, and so on.

If you choose option 3, just be careful. This is science, and there is a right answer. If it obviously sounds right, then you should be fine. But if your efforts are questionable, then skip the effects. Clean audio is never bad. Clean audio is always a right answer.

Music

Selecting the right music and watching someone score your film live are two of the most rewarding experiences an editor can have. If you're working with a major budget, editing a big-time movie, or just have money to blow, hiring a music supervisor and composer is a really good idea. But in modern-day editing, one person is usually expected to do it all. That's where you come in.

Selecting Music

The most important rule of music selection is that your personal tastes don't matter. Chances are, your favorite song isn't going to make it into any of your films—and there's a good chance you couldn't afford it anyway. On the other hand, music selection is a really good way to acquire an identity as an editor. Just make sure your own taste doesn't get in the way of what's best for the film.

If you're lucky—really, really lucky—you know a great composer who will play music for any film you do. But if you're like the rest of us, you're using third-party websites to pick music. Selecting music is a very free-spirited game in which you can almost do whatever you want. What I share here is the playbook that has helped me win Best Original Score for several films I've had in film festivals.

Four Rules of Music in Film

Whether you follow all of these rules, or none of them, let these thoughts on music selection guide you in making the best choices for your story. The music can be a major differentiator in the viewers' experience of your film.

1. TRY MANY SOURCES

Many third-party music websites offer a vast array of music styles and price ranges. You shouldn't be loyal to just one of them. You're limiting yourself by saying, "This is the site I use for music." When it comes to music, the last thing you want to do is be repetitive. Where you look also depends on what exactly you're looking for.

A *score* is music that is built like a story with the arc right there in the music. A score doesn't repeat itself and it doesn't have lyrics. Scores are best used under dialogue, or in scenes leading up to dialogue. You probably wouldn't use a score for a montage.

A *song* is usually formulaic: It usually has three verses and a chorus, regardless of the presence of lyrics. You'd probably use a song for a montage. Sometimes editors get trapped into using *looped* songs (songs that have a repetitive format) as score, and although it can work, it's not the best option. When editing wedding and event videos, people often tend to select a song to edit to. Editing to a song entails selecting your music before you edit and then making your cuts based on music (and music alone) as opposed to selecting the music after a rough cut of the edit is created. Editing to a song can work, don't get me wrong, but using a score makes for a much more dynamic feeling in the final film.

My advice is to find three or four go-to music websites so you have diverse offerings. My absolute favorite is www.AudioNetwork.com, which features a great mix of scores and allows you to search according to mood, feel, genre, or random. You can also separate songs into individual tracks. Let's say you find a song you love, but you don't like the drums. On this site, you can take them out. That's unique! Other sites I like are www.Audiojungle.com and www.TripleScoopMusic.com.

2. DON'T SELECT MUSIC FIRST

Music is important, but you shouldn't select it first. That's right. Raise your hand if you're guilty of sitting down to start your editing process, and the first thing you do is pick the music. You need to break that bad habit. By picking the music first, you're giving music way too much power. Besides, you can't pick music for something that doesn't exist.

Edit your films to the point of full rough cuts and *then* pick music. This makes selecting the music for a film an easier and shorter process. For example, say a film is mostly dialogue. That pretty much eliminates any songs with lyrics, hard drums, or anything else that may overcrowd the narrative.

Another problem with selecting music first is that it can influence the length of the piece. It happens all the time. An editor starts to edit a web commercial and picks a song that's two minutes and 24 seconds long. So the commercial ends up being that length. That's way too convenient.

> **TIP** *Your film should be as long as it is good, not as long as the song you picked.*

3. DON'T LET MUSIC DICTATE YOUR CUTS

Cutting to the music is the single most overrated and overused concept in film editing. In order of priority, here is what should be dictating your cut points:

1. **Pacing:** Whatever the best timing of the cut is.

2. **Characters:** Using the narrative perspective, characters can often indicate a cut point.

3. **Hiding a mistake:** Editors are the people who make everyone else look good (and get no credit for it). If an actor sneezes while his character is giving a speech, you will need to cut out the sneeze and cover the cut points with B-roll or a cutaway shot.

4. **Sound:** Sound sometimes dictates cut points (discussed later in this chapter). Sound can influence a cut point for several reasons, including justifying the existence of a sound. Sometimes you need to cut to the visual source of a sound.

5. **Music:** Last, and very much the least of your worries as an editor, is cutting *to* the music.

I'm not saying that you should *never* cut to the music. If you're working on a music video or a montage, by all means try it. It might be your best option. Just don't lean on it. After you edit the rough cut and then lay down your music, it's OK to change cut points to synchronize with the music, but don't stress over it. Cutting to music can become a crutch.

> **TIP** *Make the best film you can without music, and then add music to enhance the film.*

4. MUSIC DOES NOT CREATE MOOD; IT ONLY ENHANCES IT

The idea that music enhances—rather than creates—mood is hard to swallow. I'm sure some people will disagree, but I'll attempt to prove my case. Think about it: If music created mood, then all scenes would need music to have mood. We know for a fact that's not true. Plenty of scenes have no music but viewers still feel the emotion.

An example that sticks out in my head is in the movie *Déjà Vu*. Denzel Washington's character starts freaking out and throwing chairs because he can't get a straight answer to a simple question. It's a classic Denzel blow-up moment, and it has no music in the background.

The point is, characters and the story create the mood. Music can only come in and enhance the mood.

For the last wedding video I ever edited, I used music that I heard in an NBA playoff ad campaign, and it worked quite well. Now, if music creates mood, how is it creating the mood of a wedding and the intensity of an NBA playoff game? It isn't, and it can't. It's just taking on the context of the moment. That's what music does. It either doesn't work and destroys the moment, or it takes on the context in which it's placed.

Further Thoughts on Audio

When you edit a film that has no script, such as a documentary or live event, the editor is in control of what the audio communicates. In that case, think of the rough cut of your film as the "script writing" process that never took place. If you have free rein with the project, the order in which events take place is totally up to you. You can even reorder a character's sentences.

Don't worry about the visuals right away. Instead, focus on crafting the world's best "audiobook." Once you can *hear* the story, then go back to the beginning and tell the story visually. For example, let's say you have two 20-minute interviews for a roughly seven-minute documentary film you're creating. The first thing you do is what's called a *breakdown*. Basically, you choose the best sound bites from the interview that tell the story you want to tell. The order in which they are placed and what you choose to include is what makes you the storyteller. Once you select the elements you want to use to tell the story, then focus on telling that story visually. Then you can top it off with some specialized audio techniques as discussed in this chapter.

Audio: Clean or Relative to Distance?

Recording sound *clean* means recording the actual sound. You use a process similar to recording dialogue: Get the mic close to the sound source and maintain the mic at a constant distance throughout the recording. The idea is to create *natural sound,* which is sound that falls somewhere between sound effects and ambient audio. For example, let's say that a car door closing is a sound effect while the street noise is ambient sound. A car seen entering would be a natural sound.

When you record natural sound, you have two options. You can record it relative to its distance from the camera or you can record it clean. There is no right or wrong answer here. It depends on your approach. I'll share the pros and cons of each method and let you be the judge.

RECORDING SOUND RELATIVE TO DISTANCE

I record sound relative to distance most of the time. What does recording sound relative to distance mean? Think of the camera as the viewer. Where you place it, how you move it, and how the viewers hear the sound all affect the viewing experience. When viewers see a person running, the main sound they expect is feet smacking the ground. Should the sound be a constant, clean sound of running? Or should it be relative to the character's (viewer's) distance from the camera?

The opening credit sequence to *The Social Network* consists of shots of the main character running to his dorm room. As he runs toward the camera, the sound of his shoes gets louder. As he runs away from the camera, the sound gets softer. This represents real life—as if the viewers are standing right there. That's why I favor sound as relative to distance in most cases.

For something like running or a car alarm going off, this method works. Say you start with a wide shot of someone running and then cut to a close-up of the feet. Should the sound be louder? With this particular approach, yes. Not only does the visual draw you in, but so does the sound.

> **NOTE** *When recording voices, recording sound relative to distance is a big no-no.*

RECORDING CLEAN

You can never go wrong by recording something clean (on its own, with a microphone) because you can always make it sound closer or farther away in postproduction. But if you record natural sound at its actual distance during a shot, that can never be changed. Recording sound clean is always the safest bet. For me, though, something about the organic sound of a distant footstep is alluring. I never feel like I can duplicate the distance to be as accurate sounding as I want it to be.

If you ask the other school of thought—for example, a filmmaker such as Michael Bay—he's going to tell you that my opinion is wrong. (Again, I'm not sure this is a case of right and wrong as much as it is a case of difference of approach.) In his movie *Transformers,* normal-looking cars unfold into giant robots. Anytime something transforms, no matter its distance from the camera, the sound is clean as if you were a fly on the transformer itself.

Cutting On Loud Sounds

FIGURE 6.5 shows what an audio wave looks like on the timeline. The highest point in the wave is called a *peak*. The peak is the biggest spike in the wave. In editing software, the bottom half of the timeline will have all the audio, and the top half will have all the video clips. The audio waves can be very useful in situations like editing a music video. You can see where the peaks will be and make cuts based on those peaks. You can easily spot the loudest sounds on the timeline because they are the highest peaks on the audio wave.

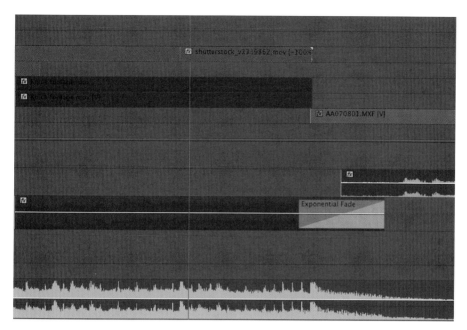

FIGURE 6.5 From this audio wave, you may choose a peak as a possible cut point.

Whenever I see a spike in an audio wave, I ask myself if that can be a cut point. Why? Because of something called the *corneal reflex*. This is an involuntary blinking of the eyelids in response to sounds greater than 40–60 decibels. A *decibel* (dB) is a measurement of power used to determine the volume (loudness) of a particular sound when it's played through a speaker. Decibels don't quite control volume like the remote on your TV; dB is simply a universal standard of measuring sound. For the purposes of editing, think of decibels as power, which relates to volume.

It's happened to you a million times. A door slams in your face. A hammer hits a nail. You drive with the windows down on a nice day and stop at a construction site where they are using a jackhammer. These sounds make you blink.

When you spot these loud sounds in your films—whether it's a gun shot or a teacup being placed on a table loudly—you should be salivating at the idea that this is an invincible cut point. Why is it invincible? If the viewer blinks, they didn't even see the cut happen. As you go through your editing, try to identify these moments because when they happen, you want to capitalize on them.

Audio Transitions

Audio transitions come in two flavors, and you will use them all the time. An *exponential fade* is a gradual fade to silence. A *constant power fade* (or *gain fade*) is a gradual fade to –3 decibels. You are likely to use one of these fades between many audio clips.

When you fade two audio clips together for any reason, you will use a constant power fade. The most common reason to crossfade two audio clips together is that the room tone in the background is at different levels. (Audio crossfade works the same as video crossfade does, gradually fading out one clip while fading in another.) Instead of cutting from one clip to the other, which sounds choppy, you crossfade the two so the audience doesn't detect a change. You use a constant power fade because the audio doesn't go silent during that kind of fade. The two blend together without any dead air.

When you fade in or out from silence, use the exponential fade because it fades into and out of silence (0 dB). When editing audio, the most important thing is for it to be smooth. What does that mean, and how does it relate to fades? When a film starts, audio often fades in from silence. Even if you don't hear the gradual fade, it's there. Sometimes, you'll even fade in something as simple as room tone. Remember, room tone is not silent, and when room tone just starts without a fade, it's jarring. Whenever a scene or film starts fading up from nothing, you need to ease the viewer into the sound. You use an exponential fade for this because it gradually fades up from nothing.

Using a constant gain fade lets you fade two audio clips together without a discernible change from one audio clip to the other. Imagine you're crossfading the audio from a wide shot to a medium shot in the same scene. (As you might remember, the room tone in the wide shot will be louder than from the medium shot because the mic is much farther away from the character. The mic being farther away forced you to raise the recording volume, thus raising the background room tone.) If you cut from the wide shot to the medium shot, the viewers will hear the dramatic change in room tone—a mistake. Instead, you crossfade the audio only, from the wide to the medium, so there is a gradual, undetectable change in the room tone. For that, you need to use the constant power fade—because the constant power fade never goes silent. If you use the exponential fade, the sound would actually go silent for a brief second. Therein lies the difference between the two fades.

No matter what you are editing, you will use a lot of audio transitions to get from one clip of audio to the next.

Starting the Edit with Audio Help

Many films start with the audio first, and then follow with the video. Even when a film starts with a black screen, sometimes we can hear the sounds of the film. In the film *Moneyball,* the credits start and you can hear the game announcers before the visual starts. This is very common.

It comes back to the viewers participating in the storytelling process. Because they can hear what's happening, it gives them time to imagine the visuals and it gets them involved in the story. You can also use audio to create anticipation.

As long as you're using a sound that's in the story, such as a gun shot or the sound of a car crash, then bringing the audio in early can help create anticipation. It should be a sound that draws attention to itself. Remember the person walking down a dark hallway in the discussion on narrative perspective in Chapter 3? What if you add eerie sound effects that get louder and louder as the character walks farther down the hallway. That's another way to get the viewers to participate in the storytelling process.

> **TIP** *The sounds can be nothing but the wind, but if you use them to get the viewers asking themselves questions, you own them.*

Consider this example: Maybe you're working on a wedding film with a narrative driven by a speech at the reception. Rather than start the visuals of the reception and the person talking, try telling the story in order with the audio of the speech as the narrative. When you get to the reception, you finally show the person who's been speaking the whole time. It's like a mini reveal (as discussed in Chapter 1), but it creates the illusion that things have been completely tied together.

Always remember, the audio is just as important as the visual. It's not something that just goes along with the visual. It, too, needs to be approached with the same thought process as visual editing.

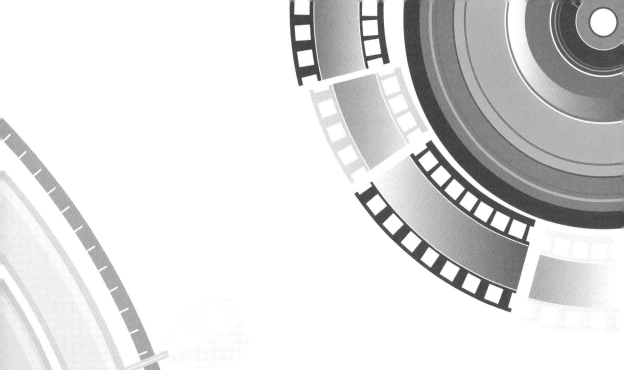

CHAPTER 7

The Editing Process

Now that you know how to think about editing, it's time to learn the process. Let me say up-front that the process I've developed over the years is geared more toward unscripted films. However, this process has its place in scripted films, although you may skip a few parts of the process covered here in this chapter. The end goal remains the same. In the editing process, the major difference between scripted and unscripted projects is that you know the order of the narrative (or at least have a base to work from) with a script. With unscripted, you're basically "scripting" the story while you edit.

When the tasks hamper your creativity, you're severely hindering your final film's potential.

The editing process is strategically designed to front-load the editing with the tasks that don't require creativity. The creative parts are bunched together at the back end of the editing process. This is my own personal process, and it's geared toward what *I* think is important. I'll warn you: My process is a little weird. You don't have to follow it. Feel free to stick to your own process, if you have one, or develop your own. However, I believe that my process, invented in the digital age, is appropriate for the digital age. It quantifies creativity for the editor by clustering all the creative parts together.

When you edit, it's easy to feel like you can never just sit down and create. Instead, you're worrying about where this particular clip is or finding that particular shot. When the tasks hamper your creativity, you're severely hindering your final film's potential—and you may not even know it.

> **TIP** Remember, creativity is a flow. In the flow of creativity, great ideas are born. Being bogged down with organizational tasks, workflow problems, and other editing process headaches while trying to be creative is not the way to achieve maximum creative output.

Beginning Again… at the Beginning

The first step to becoming a great editor is asking the right questions. The first question you should be asking is: "Where does editing begin?" The answer is: with organization. Getting and staying organized comes with practice; to be disciplined, you may need to constantly remind yourself of the payoff. Everything about the editing *process* is designed to expedite the physical craft. In that vein, you will want to remove any possible distractions, detours, or problems you may encounter during that process.

Let's face it: You edit on a computer. And whenever you depend on a computer, you're bound to run into technical issues, especially when you're putting the type of strain on the processor that editing does. Remaining organized and having a clear plan of attack helps eliminate roadblocks. (And these roadblocks *will* crop up if you choose to skip the planning and organizing phase.) Even if planning and organizing seems tedious and time consuming, down the road you'll be glad you did it. The whole purpose of organization is to keep from interrupting your flow while you're in the editing groove.

Once you understand that editing is more of an art than a technical skill, you'll realize that becoming inspired and getting into a rhythm are ultra-important. Think about editing like you think about working out. Organization is the pre-workout stretch. If you work out without stretching, you're more likely to pull a muscle. If you stop to answer the phone in the middle of a workout, then talk for 20 minutes, that's a huge interruption in the workout. Interruptions like this make you lose focus.

When it comes to video editing, staying organized means staying focused.

Step 1: Don't Do Anything!

Yes, you read that right. The first step in every project is to do nothing but think. Thinking is your greatest weapon, and documenting those thoughts is how you stay on course. In every editing session you will be in one of two different situations: working off a script or crafting a story out of footage (yours or someone else's). Regardless of the situation, the process does not change—ever. Every editor's first step is the same. You need to ask yourself the all-important question:

What's the story?

If you can't answer that question, get up, go for a run or bike ride, play video games—whatever relaxes your mind. The one thing you should *not* do is edit. If you don't know what the story is, editing is like a rocking chair: It gives you something to do, but it doesn't get you anywhere.

TIP You can compare editing to constructing a building. (This analogy comes into play when we explore the concept of narrative bases later in this chapter.) When constructing a building, you work off a blueprint—your idea, concept, or script. Make sure you have a blueprint and follow it as you go. Of course, changes are made, ideas evolve, and stories develop, but you can't evolve something from nothing (at least in editing). There must be some tangible idea as a starting point.

I hope I've made myself clear: You should not actually edit until you know the story. If you need help identifying the story, write down the five plot points in the story arc as discussed in Chapter 1. Try to write a one-sentence description of each part of the arc: exposition, rising action, climax, falling action, and resolution. From there, you can use the five plot points to categorize footage. Once the story is established, whether your project is scripted or unscripted, you can proceed with the second step.

▶ FINDING THE STORY

To find the story, you may need to analyze the five plot points. Here's an example from a documentary I worked on.

- **Exposition:** In 1980, Dwight Anderson is the greatest high school basketball player to ever live and is a sure first-round pick in the NBA draft. Instead, he chooses to go to school at the University of Kentucky after being recruited by Leonard Hamilton.

- **Rising action:** Dwight is a star in college and grabs the attention of all NBA scouts. He leads the Kentucky Wildcats to the NCAA tournament as a number two seed. In the Sweet 16, he breaks his arm and is lost for the tournament. During the off-season, Dwight unexpectedly transfers to the University of Southern California (USC).

- **Climax:** Dwight picks up a terrible drug habit and gets thrown out of school. Even with his widely known habit, he's drafted by the NBA, but he never reports.

- **Falling action:** After a long battle with drug addiction and several run-ins with the law, Dwight enters rehab at age 50.

- **Resolution:** Dwight is clean. He plays in an old-timers' league with several retired basketball Hall of Famers, and he still dominates every aspect of the game.

Step 2: Logging and Labeling Preliminaries

Let's say you film an event and just drop the footage on a 500 GB hard drive. Due to the crazy shooting schedule, and everything else you have going on in your life, you don't bother to change the filenames. The original filenames are often something like MXF 4942, which is not very helpful. Such a filename tells you nothing about the contents of the clip—and therefore it can be very frustrating to wade through those clips to find the ones you need. This is why you need to do some organization and file management.

Using Evernote and Note-Taking Software

How do you go about logging and labeling all those clips so you can start working with them? First, you need some type of note-taking software. I recommend Evernote. Evernote is a free online service that syncs to all your devices in real time. This means you can use the Evernote app to jot down ideas whenever they come to you. You can add your notes from your smartphone, and they're right there waiting for you when you get home. This universal, 24/7 access is why I use Evernote as opposed to, say, a Microsoft Word document. **FIGURE 7.1** shows a sample of what a logging session in Evernote looks like.

```
GET IN MOTION TOUR TRAILER (GPS)


BIN_BEFORE PHONE CALL

    CLIP 9697_CU_JOHNNY'S FEET_ROCKING BACK AND FOURTH
    CLIP 9698_W_JOHNNY READING BOOK_ROCKING BACK AND FOURTH
    CLIP 9698_M_JOHNNY READING BOOK_REACHES FOR PHONE AND FALLS (STRAIGHT ON)
    CLIP 9698_W_JONNY REACHING FOR PHONE AND FALLING_SIDE VIEW
    CLIP 9699_M_PHONE RINGING
    CLIP 9700_CU_PHONE RINING

BIN_PHONE CALL (DIALOGUE)

    CLIP 9701_M_JOHNNY SAYS LINES
    CLIP 9702_M_JOHNNY SAYS LINES _BEST TAKE
    CLIP 9703_EXC_LIPS_JOHNNY SAYS "VIDEO?"
    CLIP 9704_M_UP ANGLE_JOHNNY SAYS LINES

BIN_CLAY LINES

    CLIP 9705
```

FIGURE 7.1 These project notes, recorded in Evernote, list the scene name at the top. The clip numbers follow with a one-line description of what's happening in each clip.

Evernote also has a feature called *group notebooks*. Group notebooks are key when you're working in a group. Many studios have several people working on a project at the same time, and the Evernote group notebook is a great way to share ideas. Evernote isn't the only tool in the shed, though. Google Docs offers similar features, and there are others. Because I use Evernote personally, I can speak for its reliability. You can certainly use other note-taking and collaborative systems.

Asset Management: Browsing Footage with Thumbnails

The second thing you need is a program for browsing and managing your footage. Hands down, Adobe Bridge is your best bet. The reason Bridge works so well is that it allows direct access to your actual files. Applications such as Expression Media only allow access through their own workflow. When you change the name of a file in Bridge, for example, it changes the actual filename on your hard drive. (In most cases, that's not a good thing because you normally don't want to change the filenames yet, but in this case, it's exactly what you want to do if you plan on changing the filenames of your clips.) The wisdom of how and when to change filenames depends on the type of project you're doing. If you're doing a documentary with hundreds of hours of footage, it may behoove you to change *Clip 001* to *Lawyer Interview* in hopes that it helps you organize. If you're doing a smaller project, changing each filename is a waste of time.

Another option is Red Giant's BulletProof. With BulletProof, you can create groups, organize clips, and even perform a simultaneous backup of the files while importing. You can use BulletProof instead of Bridge or in addition to Bridge. Ingesting (importing) your files from the CF or SD card you shot on through BulletProof is always a good idea. If you don't have access to any program that does browsing, using a file viewer such as Windows Explorer or the Mac Finder works OK as well, as shown in **FIGURE 7.2.**

At the end of the day, you need to watch the clips and take notes. Bridge and Bullet Proof are made for that specific purpose, so they make the process a little easier. If you don't have them, it's not a game changer. You just need to do a little more work by hand.

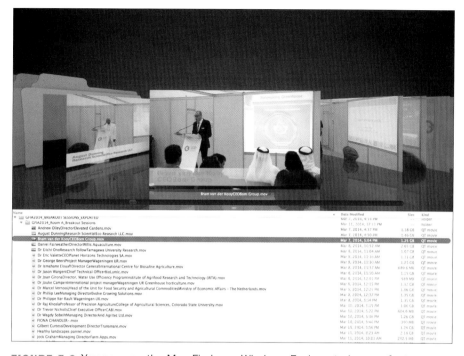

FIGURE 7.2 You can use the Mac Finder or Windows Explorer to browse footage.

Step 3: Downloading Footage

After you finish a shoot—whether it be a wedding, event, commercial, music video, or movie scene—you have to *download* (sometimes called *ingest*) the footage from the camera to a hard drive.

It is still not a good idea to change the names of the original files at this point. Your only mission right now is to back up the files. Make sure you have copies in at least two places. When working with video files, you must accept the fact that external hard drives are a part of your project budget. The files you accumulate are far too big to store on your computer's internal hard drives. Each project should have two external hard drives. One is your main drive, and the other is a backup hard drive.

> **TIP** If your files don't exist in two places, they don't exist. Always, always *back up* your files so you have two copies in two different places.

To get the files on your computer, your best bet is to simply drag and drop the files into a Finder window or Windows Explorer window for the selected hard drives. One caveat: Don't attempt to download to your main external drive and your external backup drive at the same time. This may seem faster, but it's not. You're actually doubling the wait time of the download. If you drop the footage files onto both external drives at the same time, you're splitting the speed of the CF or CD card in half. It's more efficient to copy files to one drive, and then copy them to the other drive.

Step 4: Labeling Folders

Once your footage is downloaded in two places, you need to start relabeling the folders. When you record on a CF or SD card, the camera puts the video files in folders. After a day of shooting, you may have as many as three or four folders. If you ran a few cameras, you could have ten folders. It's important to give these folders names that you'll understand, as opposed to the unhelpful names the camera gives them. To rename a folder in the Mac Finder, click on it, press Return, and type a new name. In the Windows Explorer, right-click the folder, select Rename, and type a new name. Be sure to do this before you copy the files to your backup drive so you don't have to do it twice. Have no fear, your files are on the main hard drive, and they're still on the cards they were recorded on. They still exist because they are still in two places.

If the director or cinematographer in the field does a good job of staying organized, you'll likely have each scene on a separate card or cards. Let's say they didn't do a good job—or you're organizing footage from an event—and the footage is just scattered randomly on cards in no particular order. That's OK, because you will move those folders into bins and sub-bins once they are imported into the editing program. *Bins* are just another name for folders in the editing program. These are different from the folders on your hard drive. *Sub-bins* are like subfolders inside folders.

Let's say you have two cards with video footage, and one card with external audio files. Label the cards something like this:

    NAME OF THE SHOOT_VIDEO FILES_NAME OF THE CAMERA_CARD 1

    NAME OF THE SHOOT_VIDEO FILES_NAME OF THE CAMERA_CARD 2

    NAME OF THE SHOOT_AUDIO FILES_CARD 1

This doesn't tell you what's specifically in those folders on the hard drive, but that's OK. Right now, you're just getting rid of the useless folder names the camera provides. It's most likely not going to help you in terms of organizing the content, but it does help to reference the camera it was shot with. Maybe you are shooting with three different cameras, one of which is the main camera. With this type of labeling, you will know where all the footage from each camera is. Or, maybe you have three shooters and you want to add a person's name to the end of the label. Maybe you know who the best shooters are or where they were positioned during the shoot. Now you know where to find that footage.

Once you rename the folders, you can copy the folders to your backup drive. Store the backup drive in a safe place, but not too far away—you will want to back up any additional files along with the sequence once the editing is complete.

Let's review the labeling process up to now:

1. Copy the footage from your cards to an external hard drive.

2. Rename the footage folders once the copying is complete.

3. Back up the folders that contain the footage to a second external hard drive; store the drive in a safe place.

Step 5: Logging Bins

After backing up your files, create a project in your video editing software. Within the software, use the same labeling system for every file you create for each project you're working on. It should match the folder names in a similar way. In this instance, the name of the project file would be:

NAME OF THE PROJECT_THE YEAR_YOUR NAME

You never know when you might have to reopen this project, or who else might open it, so be sure all your labels are self-explanatory. I like to use a very simple rule: If I die and someone has to take over the project, he or she should have no trouble navigating through the files.

Now you will import your labeled footage folders into your video editing software. The procedures may differ from program to program. In Adobe Premiere, it's as simple as dragging each folder into the main project bin, as shown in **FIGURE 7.3**.

FIGURE 7.3 In the Adobe Premiere screen, you drag content into the bottom-left section. The footage is then accessible within the program.

Once the files are imported into the program, you're ready to begin the logging phase. *Logging* consists of watching all of your footage and becoming familiar with it. While logging, you will create bins and sub-bins so that the project has its own method of organization. This needs to be much more detailed than what's on the drive. The drive contains the folders you renamed when you copied the footage, but those folders provide minimal information about the footage. The bins you create inside your video editing software should be more detailed and cite specific scenes or moments.

Here's an example of a folder name on the hard drive:

NAME OF THE SHOOT_VIDEO FILES_NAME OF THE CAMERA_CARD 1

And here's an example of a folder name inside your video editing program:

NAME OF THE SHOOT_DWIGHT INTERVIEW_CAMERA A

After the footage is imported, you can start watching footage and creating bins. Let's assume you filmed a wedding and are looking to get your project organized. The footage is copied, backed up, and imported into the project. Let's say the first clip you watch is of the bride putting on her wedding dress. You would create a new bin by right-clicking (Windows) or Control-clicking (Mac) in the space where you dropped the original folders in, choosing Create New Bin, and labeling that bin Bride Getting Ready. You would drop that clip into the bin you just created and then continue watching footage. Every time you see a clip of the bride getting ready, you drop it into that bin. Every time you find a clip that didn't belong in that bin, create a new bin that describes that scene or moment. By the time you get through all the footage, all the clips should be in different bins.

Creating In and Out Points

In and out points essentially identify the usable points of a clip. Let's assume you have 1,000 or so clips. The first clip I watch is a shot of people arriving at the event. I'm going to do two things when I see this. First, I'll create in and out points for the clip. In any editing program, you can create nondestructive in an out points that basically *trim* the clip so that only the parts you want go into the timeline. **FIGURE 7.4** shows a clip with in and out points.

In the top left of the video editing program screen, you see an image called the *source screen.* The source screen is where you watch all of your clips. The top-right window is where you play the film you are editing on the timeline. At the very bottom of the source screen, notice the gray bar with a lighter gray bar inside it. A yellow marker displays directly in the middle of the gray bar. The gray bar represents how long the clip is, and the lighter gray bar that starts with the yellow marker represents the *in point* of that clip. I'm only selecting that part of the clip as the part that I like. Where the lighter gray bar ends is the *out point*.

FIGURE 7.4 The Adobe Premiere interface makes it easy to view a clip's in and out points.

You can change the in and out points at any stage in the editing process—without affecting what's on the timeline. Let's say I have a one-minute clip of three people walking through a door at different times. I can create in and out points for the first person to walk in, drag them to the timeline, and then go back and create new in and out points for the second person walking through the door, and then drag them onto the timeline. At this point in the process, I'm creating big sections of in and out points. If I like all three people walking through the door, I would include all of them in my in and out points. The purpose here is when I come back to the clip later, I have some sort of reference regarding the usable sections of the clip.

Most clips have what are known as *handles*. Handles are part of the clip, but are usually part of the setup or wind-down of the shot. Usually, handles either are unusable or have no purpose in the film you're making. An example of a handle is the footage recorded before the director calls *action*, or the part of the clip that's recorded after the director calls *cut*. In an event video, it could be the part of the clip where you're still framing your shot. Most of the time, you won't use these parts of the clips. However, you never know when a facial expression, or what's known as *sample air* (remember room tone?), can be pulled from that section.

Making in and out points for the clips during the logging phase is a good idea, but it doesn't mean that you need to live by them or never look at the other sections of the clips again. You make in and out points to expedite the process later. These in and out points are nondestructive, meaning that the footage remains.

Creating Bins

The next thing you'll do after watching each clip is move it to more specifically named bins. For example, a bin label might read something like this:

NAME OF THE SHOOT_PEOPLE ARRIVING

The name now tells you what's inside the bin. Once you create a bin, you can drop your clip inside it and remove it from its original bin. For every clip you come across that falls into that category (in this case, PEOPLE ARRIVING), you place it in that bin. For every new clip you come across that doesn't fit, create a new bin to place it in. For an event I did for Expedia, the first round of organizing produced the following bins:

EXPEDIA_PEOPLE ARRIVING

EXPEDIA_PRE CON BREAKFAST

EXPEDIA_BREAKOUT SESSION 1

EXPEDIA_BREAKOUT SESSION 2

EXPEDIA_CEO KEYNOTE

EXPEDIA_PRESIDENT KEYNOTE

EXPEDIA_EMPLOYEES DURING CONFERENCE

This last bin name (EXPEDIA_EMPLOYEES DURING CONFERENCE) is very important. Why did I make a bin for these rather than just placing random clips of employees watching speeches into the sessions where they occurred? Expedia had 14 keynote speakers, and I had reaction shots from each. As far as the editing is concerned, a shot of an employee watching the CEO's keynote or the president's keynote happened where you say they happened. Once the footage is in editing, it's all about the context in which the clips are placed that decides their value. These clips are called *universal clips*. Universal clips are not to be confused with B-roll. Universal clips are still parts of the main story, but they can be used anywhere. B-roll falls more along the lines of exterior building shots.

> **TIP** *Keep this in mind during the first round of organizing because you want to store universal clips in the same bin. That way, when you are looking for a particular shot, you're not looking in a bunch of different bins to find it.*

Context is key to understanding the power of editing. I might have a shot of a guy laughing at a joke the president told in his speech, but I might use that shot during a moment when I wanted a smile from the crowd during the CEO's speech. That's what you need to think about as an editor, and that's why you must organize clips based on their possible context.

Scrubbing

When you go through the initial logging and organization process, it's a good idea to watch clips all the way through, but it's not imperative. You can do what's known as *scrubbing*. Scrubbing is when you drag the curser across the clip and gauge its potential category or bin. You can also press L on the keyboard to speed up the clip's playback. (In Adobe Premiere, speeding up a clip doesn't drop frames like older programs did.) Your primary goal in logging is to establish some rough in and out points and get every clip into a bin that represents its category.

Logging Audio

Audio files often pose the biggest challenge during the logging phase. Unlike video, there's no thumbnail that gives you a clue to what's in an audio clip. Therefore, you need to stay especially organized with audio during the filming phase. If you're shooting a wedding or a corporate event, chances are you recorded one long audio clip on an external recorder for each speaker or section. For a wedding, drop the ceremony audio file in the ceremony bin, and the speeches in the speeches bin. Use the same drill for events: Place each audio file with the matching keynote speaker.

If you recorded audio in-camera, you don't have to worry about this. If you do have long audio files and dozens of short clips, which would represent a DSLR camera setup, you can learn about syncing that audio a little later in this chapter. If your project is scripted, syncing the audio doesn't come until the very end. (Those working on scripted projects should not use a program such as PluralEyes to line up the audio for them, because doing so conflicts with the editing process.)

Lining Up Audio

After you place the clips and audio in their respective bins, the real logging happens— along with some note taking. If you recorded long audio files for events, you need to use software such as PluralEyes to *line up* that audio (that is, sync it to the video). If you do a lot of events and don't have this program, I highly recommend that you get it. If you can't afford this type of tool, you should sell lemonade on a busy street corner until you can afford one. That's how crucial it is. In all seriousness, if you don't have such a program, you'll be with the scripted editors and line up your audio last. (If you only do scripted work, don't worry about getting PluralEyes—you have no use for it and can skip to the next section, "The Logging Process.")

If you do have a program such as PluralEyes, line up (sync) the audio for every sequence that has external audio. Once the new project with the synced audio is created, close the current project, open the synced project, and begin working from that project. Move each sequence with lined-up audio into its respective bin, and you will be back where you started before lining up the audio.

Let's assume you don't have a program to line up the audio, and you're doing things the old-fashioned way. Don't panic. It's really not that hard. Here's what you do:

1. First, skim Chapter 6 to refresh your memory on how to read audio peaks. You should be able to see the wave on the timeline.

   Note: If you have external audio, remember that the camera also has lower quality audio built into the clip. You can use the camera audio for reference. The goal is to match the audio wave from the camera's audio to your external (and superior) audio.

2. Find the clip you're trying to line up audio for, and then identify a keyword or phrase in it. Maybe it's a wedding, and the bride says "I do." Now, go to the external audio and find that exact same point when the bride says "I do." Create in and out points to select that section. Now, match the audio waves on the timeline until they line up perfectly (**FIGURE 7.5**).

3. Don't trust your eye. Play the clip and listen to make sure it's lined up perfectly. You shouldn't hear any echo. If you hear both audio waves, then the alignment is off by a frame or two. You should hear only one audio wave.

4. Once you've determined everything is lined up perfectly, delete the on-camera audio from the timeline.

FIGURE 7.5 The top audio wave (blue) is the audio capture on camera, and the bottom audio wave (green) is the audio captured off camera. Note that the peaks in the wave align perfectly.

The Logging Process

Once the audio is lined up, you can forget about it and get back to logging. Open your first bin—any bin you choose—and open your note-taking program (such as Evernote). In your note taking, you should also be religious about the naming. The names should look like this:

NAME OF YOUR PROJECT_NAME OF THE BIN

CLIP NUMBER_SHORT AND BRIEF DESCRIPTION

CLIP NUMBER_SHORT AND BRIEF DESCRIPTION

When you watch each clip, make a brief description in the note-taking program that gives you an idea of what the clip is about. For example, I might use something like, "(W) People walking in." The (W) stands for wide shot, (M) stands for medium, and (CU) stands for close-up.

In your note-taking program, create a ranking system for clips and a legend that goes with it. The idea is to make a note about how good each shot is based on its cinematic properties or storytelling value. This is just more information you can use to prioritize things—it doesn't mean that you should disregard things that don't have a good ranking later in the process. You could use a color labeling system to rank each shot. Some people use a ranking system for scene separation or shot type separation, but I like to create sub-bins for shot types. I find the color labeling is most useful for a ranking system. But don't forget to clearly explain the labeling system used in your note-taking program or else it will be useless.

For the second round of logging, you have two goals in mind:

1. Document each shot on the *log* (your note-taking document). Each shot should have a color label, the name of the shot, the shot type (W, M, CU), and a brief description of what's happening in the clip. This log should serve as the "GPS" to the entire project. Someone should be able to read it and understand where the shot is, how good you think it is, what type of shot it is, and what's happening in the shot—all without looking at the actual footage. This log makes the editing process so much smoother once you get deep into the project.

2. Create sub-bins. Sub-bins make the searching process so much easier. You can create sub-bins based on shot type, with W, M, and CU as the categories you start with.

After completing two rounds of logging, your log is fully complete, your project is organized, and it's time for the dump timeline.

Step 6: Creating the Dump Timeline

The name of this process is exactly what it sounds like. You're going to be dumping clips on the timeline. While most editors do not include this task in their workflow, I highly recommend it. A dump timeline will save you time and take the guesswork out of editing. It also answers the all-important question: Where do I begin? In the days of editing film, that answer was pretty simple—the beginning. Now, it's not so simple.

This is because film editing has evolved from editing actual *film*. Most of us don't edit film anymore as digital filmmaking offers more options. This is where my title, *Out of Order,* comes from. The way I edit is in a circular process. For the dump timeline, I basically dump things on the timeline that I want to use in the story. Creating from a blank timeline can be overwhelming and intimidating—it can even curb creativity the way an empty page can intimidate a writer. The dump timeline certainly eliminates that problem.

Start with any scene or section you want and watch each clip from the bin. You could use your log to find the useful clips, but that log is really meant for organizing ideas and quickly finding clips when you're deep in the editing process. At this point, I'd almost ignore the log and consider this the third round of organization. When watching the clips, you'll make in and out points (or multiple sets of in and out points). Then drag the clips onto the timeline. In what order? It doesn't matter. How long are the clips? Irrelevant. Which tracks do I place them on? You pick. The key is to bring the clips into the timeline. Simple as that.

You accomplish two things with this process:

1. You get away from the blank timeline, which is the ultimate goal.
2. You limit the amount of footage you're working with.

Once this process is complete, you can work from the dump timeline. The only time you'll go back to the bins is for specific shots you realize you need later on. That's where the log comes in. See how that works? You're taking a really big project, organizing it, and reducing the information to about a quarter of its original size. To break it down in rough numbers, if you filmed 100 GB of footage of a wedding, organized it, and made a dump timeline, the timeline would have about 20–30 GB of footage on it. You're now crafting your story from the timeline as opposed to the raw footage of 100 GB. It simplifies things a great deal. You're now working with the prime meat.

Creating the dump timeline is no time to be stingy. If you think that a clip or a piece of a clip could be useful for any reason, bring it into the timeline. If you have five takes of the same few lines and you like four of them, bring all four to the timeline and stack them on top of each other. Stacking clips indicates that they are part of the same moment, and you'll eventually have to choose. This is not the time to decide whether a clip is too long or too short, whether something isn't exposed right, or that the audio doesn't sound good. If you rated your clips with a five-star rating system, every clip with a rating of 2.5 and higher is now on the timeline. You'll cut those down later. Right now you're just grabbing the materials you need to build your film.

> **TIP** *Creating the dump timeline should be a fast and easy process that requires very little thought. It's not the time to cut dialogue. It's not the time to select the best pieces of each clip.*

If you have a small project, such as a wedding or event, then one dump timeline should do the job. If you have a long project, then multiple dump timelines might be a good idea so you don't get overwhelmed by the mess it starts to look like. If you're working on a project that has several dump timelines, you can treat each one as a separate film and combine them later. Or, you can make all your dump timelines at once. I'd tend to choose the latter, because halfway through the editing process, you'll start to combine each dump timeline into one as it evolves. If they're not all that the same stage when you want to combine them, it can be counterproductive.

If you're working on a scripted film, the dump timeline works for you as well. For you, it's more about grabbing the best takes for each line and throwing them down on the timeline. Your dump timeline has the advantage of already being a bit more evolved and developed than something unscripted, but the philosophy is still exactly the same.

After you complete the dump timeline, it's time to evolve it into something coherent: the narrative base.

Step 7: Building the Narrative Base

The narrative base should really be its own book. It's that important. This is what the entire editing process is built around, not to mention the entire film. Everything you do before this point—logging, note taking, organizing, creating bins, and setting up the dump timeline—is all to get you to this point. All of those steps, including this one, are not the most exciting part of editing, but they're important.

Not only is the narrative base the peak of the process, it's also the foundation of the entire film. When you complete the narrative base process, you should be 60 to 70 percent done with your film, depending on the type of film you're creating.

What is a narrative base exactly? Read on.

Narrative Base in Scripted Films

For a scripted film, a narrative base is a start-to-finish cut of every line in the script (or scene) in order, placed on the timeline as a rough cut. When forming the base from the dump timeline, or creating one from scratch, you don't think about timing, pacing, rhythm, what lines to get down, pauses in the scene, audio, or anything related to detail. Note that with a scripted dialogue scene, it's OK to skip the dump timeline step because scripted dialogue has few variables. The point is, get the scene on the timeline in a rough cut format, and from there you go in and make it perfect.

Narrative Base in Documentaries

If you're making a documentary, the narrative base will be the evolution from your dump timeline. If you've done your dump timeline correctly, there should be a massive and messy sequence, or many sequences, with every possible sound bite (and visuals attached) you could possibly imagine using. From that, you're going to form a coherent and somewhat seamless narrative for the entire timeline (or several dump timelines).

You're forming the narrative story. This step is about one thing and one thing only: listening. Don't worry about the visual right now. At this point, it's all about using the words to tell your story. If you've made one massive timeline, be sure you don't get distracted by how you'll transition from one section or scene to the next. Leave holes between the sections to remind yourself that you will eventually need to bridge that gap.

For a documentary, the narrative base should consist of interviews only. If you have an interview that runs on one long clip, don't worry about taking several pieces of the same clip and cutting out sections you don't want. Think about making the audio (the dialogue) seamless from one cut to the next as if it were a book on tape. The visual is irrelevant at this point in the process. Don't worry too much about making it sound seamless, but keep that in mind while forming the base. After all, this is going to be the foundation of the entire film.

Narrative Base in Event Films

If you're filming an event, including a wedding, chances are you'll include interviews. If you do, it's the same thing as a documentary. If your event is made up of speeches or live presentations, this is the time to choose the best part of those based on the intended length of the film. Of course, this won't be the last time you cut things out. If you're intending to make a five-minute film, and you end up with a six-minute narrative base, that is totally acceptable. Remember that reality doesn't matter. The speech you're using as a narrative base can be trimmed, made more fluid, and even rearranged based on what you think sounds better. That's your goal during the narrative base process.

Narrative Base as Structure

In the editing process, your goal is to try to get the legwork done before you start to attack the artistic part. Building a solid foundation is all a part of that. The narrative base is the structure of your film. When you step back and look at your final edit, the narrative base should be the process that is holding it all together.

As I said before, the process of editing a film is very similar to constructing a building. It starts from the ground up. Think of the narrative base as the structure of the building. You'd never start adding lighting fixtures and décor before the structure was built. It's really important to first create that solid foundation first for two reasons:

- It's much easier to modify an existing timeline and structure.

- It's much easier to make changes to a film that's still in the structure phase of construction.

Let's say a building is almost complete, but I decide to embed a wall-to-wall fish tank in a wall. If the builder tells me, "That's a load-bearing wall," I'm in trouble. If I really want that fish tank, the building has to come down and I need to build a new structure from the ground up. Editing is the same way. If you get deep in the editing process, and you're trying to make things perfect as you go (adding the perfect décor and furniture), making changes is going to be hard. You'll find yourself re-editing the same sections of your film more often. Taking the base structure apart is easy. Taking an almost-finished film apart is painful. In editing, everything is connected. Once one part comes down, every part needs to be analyzed and considered for demolition.

EXAMPLE OF EDITING THE NARRATIVE BASE

When is the narrative base complete? That depends on the film you're creating. After converting the dump timeline to a narrative base, it's a good idea to review it several times. Editing is all about refining, and the process of creating the narrative base is no different. The more times you go in the circle, the more refined your base will be.

Let's take an event, for example. A few years ago I did an event film for Expedia. The keynote speaker was the president of the company, and he gave two keynote speeches that ran about two hours each. I knew that the final four-minute film would feature his keynote presentation (his speech) as the narrative base structure for the entire film. We decided that going into the filming. Because of the length of the speeches, the 12-minute recording limit of the DSLR cameras we were using, and the dozens of vantage points we wanted to get of his speeches, we knew we would need software to line up the external audio. Red Giant's PluralEyes software can line up the audio for you in a matter of minutes.

Once we lined up the audio, we had a four-hour timeline of the president of Expedia talking on stage—our dump timeline. Our first round of reviewing this four-hour presentation involved cutting out everything we knew we didn't need. That brought the base to about an hour. We cut it down to a quarter of the original size on the first round. Then we went through it again, doing the same thing with the same thought process and got it down to about 20 minutes. That was the easy part. Now we had about ten minutes from one keynote speech, and ten minutes from another. We knew that the final film should feel like one presentation—not two separate speeches (notice how we ignored reality). From the 20-minute speech, we cut it down to about eight minutes. Once we had eight minutes, then it was about refining it down to about five. That was easy enough, because we looked for lines that were redundant and lines that didn't move the story forward.

But the real key here was when we started to re-order events. We moved the section that happened at the seven-minute mark to the beginning to make it our opening. All of a sudden, that made the first two minutes of the speech irrelevant—because we didn't need an opening anymore. See how that works? By rearranging the events, we made his actual opening meaningless. After a good deal of rearranging, we had a 5:30 base.

We weren't done. Finally, it was time to turn the president into the greatest speaker in the history of mankind. We took out every unnatural pause, every stutter, every sniffle—

(continues on next page)

EXAMPLE OF EDITING THE NARRATIVE BASE *(continued)*

basically, everything that didn't scream perfect. All in all, we got rid of about 15 seconds. It's wasn't much, but it made the speech feel much shorter because it was much more fluid. At this point, we needed a break in order to attack it with a fresh mind.

We still needed to eliminate about 45 seconds. With the narrative base, sometimes you leave holes in the structure because you plan to fill them with B-roll or a montage later in the process. It sounds crazy, but it's true. The purpose of the holes is so you don't worry about connecting different plot points. For example, with Expedia, one section had a bit of a different feel from the rest of the film. By leaving a placeholder, we did not need to concern ourselves with how to transition to this section of the film while building the base. We left about a 15-second hole in the timeline as a reminder to add a transition. Filling that hole in the timeline would come later in the artistic phase of the editing process.

While this is a special case of creating a narrative base, I'm using this extreme example to illustrate that there is no rule to how many times you need to go through the dump timeline and the narrative base. The rule is: Whatever it takes. Once you have a solid foundation, you can start adding all the little extras that make a film feel *real*.

Final Thoughts

One thing about editing that will never change is that you need to have a clear idea of what you're trying to accomplish before you start editing. Back to the building analogy: All buildings, big or small, start with a blueprint. For a film, the blueprint is your idea. It's important to have that idea before the process begins.

That's why you should never sit down to edit without a clear vision of what you're trying to accomplish. If you don't have a clear vision, you can work on logging or continue watching your footage. Or, distract yourself. Go play a round of golf. Go to sleep. I play video games. As mentioned, the one thing you should *not* do is edit.

Once you do start editing, you need to be very confident in your idea and your ability as an editor. The narrative base process is not glamorous. Your film will not look good for the majority of time you're editing. You won't be able to watch the first 30 seconds and get inspired. This is why the *idea* is so important. For about 70 percent of the process, my films always look bad. Then they turn the corner to what their final form will be. Only then can I start to judge the quality.

Sometimes, ideas don't end up translating well. That's the nature of art. You may have the greatest idea since sliced bread in your mind, but when you translate it into a film, it just may not work. That's not a knock on you or your idea; it's just the way it is sometimes. It's important not to judge until you're in the last phase of editing. As you get more practice, you'll get better at translating your ideas to film, and you'll be able to spot a failed idea sooner. But reserve judgment until you start to add the artistic part of the film.

Be sure to remember all you learned in Chapter 1. The story arc drives everything. Oftentimes, if I'm working on a shorter, unscripted film—as you may well find yourself doing—I create five main bins to organize the clips. Each bin represents a part of the story arc. Within those bins I create sub-bins to further categorize things. As an editor, you want to focus on telling your story visually, so the editing process is designed in a way that gives your film a foundation centered around the story arc.

To summarize the process, first you organize the footage, log it, and build a foundation for your edit. The edit starts as a dump timeline and ends with a narrative base. This is where you formulate the story arc.

Finally, you cycle back through your narrative base, place B-roll in its proper places, and select the visuals that match the narrative. This is shot selection based on conflict. After you select your shots, and the film starts to look more and more polished, you can step back and look at the film as a whole to decide which scenes, if any, need to be rearranged based on the narrative perspective. Once that's done, the film is solidly built and can be deemed a rough cut. It's *rough* because you still need to go through it again and adjust things such as pacing and rhythm. You finalize a film with audio editing.

The editing process, as you can see, follows the chapters of the book. As you edit your next film, assemble it following these chapters. The book starts with the big picture and then goes into the smaller details. Wherever you are in the process, just focus on the step you're on with its corresponding chapter.

The last thing I want to say is that it takes practice—trial and error. Editing is art, and as with any art, the only way you're going to get better is to do it over and over again. The more you do it, the more you'll know what doesn't work. Even to this day, I still re-edit things time and time again because you can always make something better.

TIP *My last words are this: In film editing, nothing is ever done—you just have to decide when you're finished.*

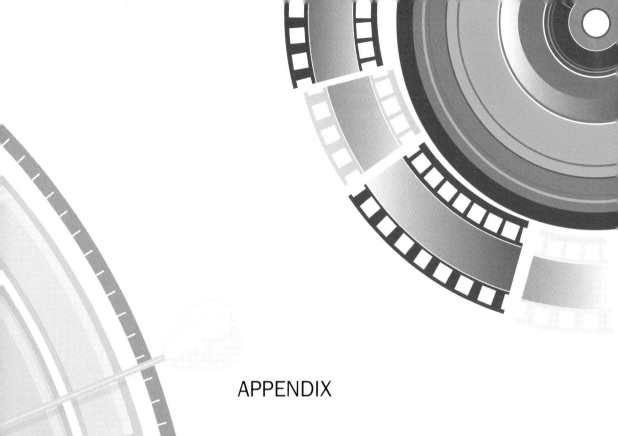

APPENDIX

Film and TV Show References

Following is a list of films and TV shows I reference in the book to illustrate a principle of editing executed at the highest level. These examples have had great influence on my personal editing style. If you watch some, or all, of these films, you'll be better able to connect them to the ideas in the book. If you can only commit to a couple, study both *The Social Network* and *Moneyball,* which execute some of the most important concepts.

21 Grams (2003)

Director: Alejandro González Iñárritu

Film Editing: Stephen Mirrione

- Chapter 3

25th Hour (2002)

Director: Spike Lee

Film Editing: Barry Alexander Brown

- Chapter 2

Any Given Sunday (1999)

Director: Oliver Stone

Film Editing: Stuart Levy, Tom Nordberg, Keith Salmon, Stuart Waks

- Chapter 2
- Chapter 4
- Chapter 5

Argo (2012)

Director: Ben Affleck

Film Editing: William Goldenberg

- Chapter 2

The Aviator (2004)

Director: Martin Scorsese

Film Editing: Thelma Schoonmaker

- Chapter 2
- Chapter 5

Babel (2006)

Director: Alejandro González Iñárritu

- Chapter 3

The Big Bang Theory (2007)

- Chapter 5

Blow (2001)

Director: Ted Demme

Film Editing: Kevin Tent

- Chapter 6

Breaking Bad (2008)

Creator: Vince Gilligan

- Chapter 1
- Chapter 2
- Chapter 3
- Chapter 4
- Chapter 5

Cocaine Cowboys (2006)

Director: Billy Corben

Film Editing: Billy Corben

- Chapter 3

Cosmos (1980)

- Chapter 3

Crash (2004)

Director: Paul Haggis

Film Editing: Hughes Winborne

- Chapter 3

The Curious Case of Benjamin Button (2008)

Director: David Fincher

Film Editing: Kirk Baxter, Angus Wall

- Chapter 3

Dallas Buyers Club (2013)

Director: Jean-Marc Vallée

Film Editing: Martin Pensa, John Mac McMurphy

- Chapter 2

The Dark Knight (2008)

Director: Christopher Nolan

Film Editing: Lee Smith

- Chapter 2

Déjà Vu (2006)

Director: Tony Scott

Film Editing: Jason Hellmann, Chris Lebenzon

- Chapter 2
- Chapter 6

Fab Five: The Texas Cheerleader Scandal (2008)

- Chapter 3

The Fast and the Furious (2001)

Director: Rob Cohen

Film Editing: Peter Honess

- Chapter 1

Fight Club (1999)

Director: David Fincher

Film Editing: James Haygood

- Chapter 1
- Chapter 2
- Chapter 3
- Chapter 4

Forrest Gump (1994)

Director: Robert Zemeckis

Film Editing: Arthur Schmidt

- Chapter 3

Game of Thrones (2011)

Creators: David Benioff, D.B. Weiss

- Chapter 2
- Chapter 5
- Chapter 6

The Godfather, Part III (1990)

Director: Francis Ford Coppola

Film Editing: Lisa Fruchtman, Barry Malkin, Walter Murch

- Chapter 6

Goodfellas (1990)

Director: Martin Scorsese

Film Editing: James Y. Kwei, Thelma Schoonmaker

- Chapter 3

Gravity (2013)

Director: Alfonso Cuarón

Film Editing: Alfonso Cuarón, Mark Sanger

- Chapter 2
- Chapter 3

Homeland (2011)

- Chapter 2

House of Cards (2013)

- Chapter 3

The Hunger Games (2012)

Director: Gary Ross

Film Editing: Christopher S. Capp, Stephen Mirrione, Juliette Welfling

- Chapter 2
- Chapter 5

Inception (2010)

Director: Christopher Nolan

Film Editing: Lee Smith

- Chapter 2
- Chapter 3

Inglourious Basterds (2009)

Directors: Quentin Tarantino

Film Editing: Sally Menke

- Chapter 4

Jaws (1975)

Director: Steven Spielberg

Film Editing: Verna Fields

- Chapter 1

Mad Men (2007)

Creator: Matthew Weiner

- Chapter 2

The Matrix (1999)

Directors: Andy Wachowski, Lana Wachowski (as The Wachowski Brothers)

Film Editing: Zach Staenberg

- Chapter 1
- Chapter 2
- Chapter 3
- Chapter 5

Moneyball (2011)

Director: Bennett Miller

Film Editing: Christopher Tellefsen

- Chapter 2
- Chapter 5
- Chapter 6

The Prestige (2006)

Director: Christopher Nolan

Film Editing: Lee Smith

- Chapter 2

Remember the Titans (2000)

Director: Boaz Yakin

Film Editing: Michael Tronick

- Chapter 2

Rocky (1976)

Director: John G. Avildsen

- Chapter 5

Sicko (2007)

Director: Michael Moore

- Chapter 3

The Social Network (2010)

Director: David Fincher

Film Editing: Kirk Baxter, Angus Wall

- Chapter 2
- Chapter 3
- Chapter 4
- Chapter 5
- Chapter 6

Star Wars (1977)

Director: George Lucas

Film Editing: Richard Chew, Paul Hirsch, Marcia Lucas

- Chapter 3

Survive and Advance (2013)

Director: Jonathan Hock

- Chapter 3

This Is the End (2013)

Directors: Evan Goldberg, Seth Rogen

Film Editing: Zene Baker

- Chapter 2

Titanic (1997)

Director: James Cameron

Film Editing: Conrad Buff, James Cameron, Richard A. Harris

- Chapter 2

The Walking Dead (2010)

Creator: Frank Darabont

- Chapter 1

Wedding Crashers (2005)

Director: David Dobkin

Film Editing: Mark Livolsi

- Chapter 5

The Wire (2002)

Creator: David Simon

- Chapter 2

Index